# The Triumph and Tragedy of

# Riddick Bowe

### Christian Vick

Llumina
Press

© 2011 Christian Vick

All rights reserved. No part of this publication may be reproduced or transmitted in any form or by any means electronic or mechanical, including photocopy, recording, or any information storage and retrieval system, without permission in writing from both the copyright owner and the publisher.

Requests for permission to make copies of any part of this work should be mailed to Permissions Department, Llumina Press, 7101 W. Commercial Blvd., Ste. 4E, Tamarac, FL 33319.

ISBN: 978-1-60594-719-8 ( PB )

Printed in the United States of America by Llumina Press

Library of Congress Control Number: 2011912665

*In loving memory of Eddie Futch, Arturo Gatti, Vernnon Forrest, and Alexis Arguello*

# The Triumph and Tragedy of

# Riddick Bowe

# 1
# Riddick Bowe Origins

Riddick Lamont Bowe was born to Dorothy Bowe in Brooklyn, New York, on August 10,1967. He was the twelfth of thirteen children. Riddick Bowe and his siblings were raised by their single mother who worked at a nearby plastic bottle factory in the Brownsville section of the borough. Riddick Bowe grew up amid poverty, drugs, and constant danger. Dorothy Bowe did everything she could to steer her children away from the temptation of the street, working the graveyard shift, preaching good morals and solid character. Riddick Bowe avoided the trappings of crime and drugs. Brownsville, Brooklyn, at the time was considered one of the worst ghettos in the city of New York. Brownsville was a commercial for resistance and struggle. Brownsville is famous for its violence; it was also famous for something else

While in middle school, a young Riddick Bowe had seen a tape of Muhammad Ali. He saw this young African American spouting poetry and throwing punches. He saw a worldwide figure famous for his diction and humor. He saw a warrior that seemed to represent all people, black or white. Seeing this tape changed Riddick Bowe's life. It gave him a dream, something to believe in. Inner-city children rarely see something so influential, so powerful, that it gives them the strength to rise above their dilapidated beginnings. Riddick Bowe was lucky enough to have such an epiphany. After awhile, he began researching Ali, watching him, studying him. One day at school, a fellow classmate contended that Joe Frazier was a better fighter than Riddick's beloved Ali. This debate evolved into a fight. A teacher in the school, who had witnessed the fight, pointed out to Riddick that he was pretty good with his hands. Since Riddick at this point was already a big fan of Ali, it was only natural he try his hand in boxing. Brownsville, Brooklyn, had produced its share of boxing talents. Floyd Patterson, the former undisputed heavyweight champion, was a Brownsville product. Iron Mike Tyson, who was actually Riddick Bowe's sixth grade classmate, would also go on to win the lineal heavyweight championship. Both men set the record for youngest man to hold the title at the time that they won it. Riddick Bowe started his boxing career with low expectations and big dreams. In boxing, he found a way to stay off the streets, away from the drug dealers. He also found a way to escape his poverty-stricken beginnings. Riddick enjoyed a stellar start to his boxing career, winning four New York Golden Gloves championships. He won those titles at different weights as his body began to fill out. He competed in the national Golden Gloves in 1985, losing a tough decision. Riddick Bowe, by the time he was nineteen, was one of the most decorated amateurs in the United States. After discussing it with his mother, he made the decision to chase his dream. He would compete for a spot on the 1988 Olympic team. Seoul, South Korea, was the sight of the 1988 Olympic Games. Riddick Bowe qualified with ease.

Riddick Bowe made quite a splash at the 1988 Olympics. Taking a page out of his Ali's book, Riddick Bowe captivated the media with his humor and impersonations. Not everybody was impressed. The boxing insiders that were in Korea for the Olympics were a bit disenchanted with Riddick's passion to win. Rumors began to circulate that he was lazy and unmotivated. These rumors grew louder as the tournament progressed. Despite the fact that Riddick was winning his fights. The negativity crested in the gold medal round when a Canadian heavyweight named Lennox Lewis stopped Riddick Bowe on his feet, seizing the super heavyweight gold medal. Many saw Riddick's effort as listless and an embarrassment. It would prove to be the defining moment of Riddick Bowe's young career. In the wake of the loss, he was seen as a bust. A waste of time, and a surefire failure. A gold medal could have helped Riddick set the world on fire; a silver medal got him nothing. When he returned home from the Olympic Games, Riddick Bowe hoped to see hundred of fans in the airport waiting to welcome their hero home. Instead, the only people at the airport were his family. After some soul-searching and downtime with his family. Riddick Bowe knew that the time had come to turn pro. He had recently fathered a child and needed means to support the newest member of his family. None of the major promoters were interested in taking Bowe on. It seemed at first that Riddick would have some difficulty getting his career off the ground.

Riddick's saving grace would come in the form of Eugene "Rock" Newman. Rock had worked for famed promoter Butch Lewis. He was eager to promote a fighter himself. After meeting with Riddick and working out an agreement, he officially turned pro. Riddick Bowe was about take take a journey, a journey that would take him to the top of the boxing world.

# 2

# Lionel Butler

The prospect known as Riddick Bowe made his professional debut on March 6, 1989, in the "Biggest Little City" in the world, Reno, Nevada. His purse would be two thousand US dollars. The fight took place at the Lawlor Events Center on the undercard of the Hector Camacho-Ray "Boom Boom" Mancini junior welterweight title fight. Riddick Bowe weighed in officially at 226 pounds; his opponent, Lionel Butler, weighed in at 202 pounds, twelve pounds north of a cruiserweight. The anticipated debut would come amidst the usual buzz that follows an Olympic medalist. Specifically a United States medalist. Given the well-documented professional success of the U.S. boxing team in 1984 (the United States boycotted the 1980 Olympics due to the Soviet Communist aggression) and the fact that the team in 1976 produced a plethora of professional talent, Riddick had no choice but to produce at a high level. Negative or positive, this generated a buzz around the young American. The buzz, however, seemed to center around what this prospect lacked as opposed to what he possessed. Respected sports journalist Ken Denlinger, of the *Washington Post*, wrote,

> **As Olympic heavyweight champion, the gold medal draped around his neck, Bowe could have stepped immediately from the ring onto Madison Avenue. Unfortunately for him, a lackluster performance against Canadian Lennox Lewis turned gold into silver. From Bowedacious to Ridiculous Bowe.**

Perhaps this was all due to him failing to capture a gold medal in South Korea during the summer of 1988, as mentioned by Ken Denlinger in his piece. Or as Rock Newman surmised, it could have been due to his fun-loving personality in an era defined by Mike Tyson and the pure rage that was his boxing persona. The unsavory word on the street that stuck to Riddick could have been a perfect confluence of these two facts. There was something else that would trouble Riddick stock. Riddick, during the Olympics, and before that, had fathered a reputation for lacking the work ethic needed to rise to the top of the heavyweight heap. The fact that he was so talented compounded the frustration of the boxing community. The loud whispers in boxing corners centered on his day-to-day machinations in training camp. Roadwork resistance and cupcake gorging were among the accusations. Riddick's "hakuna matata" attitude gave those allegations base. Much of the rumors were overblown. The gossip was a result of fearing the unknown. People were unsure of what Riddick would become. The expedient thing to do was to label him a bust before he even had the chance to become one. Riddick, very early in his boxing life, was forced to fight an uphill battle against the industry before he even threw a professional punch. No matter what anyone said; however, his physical talent and dimensions seemed to know no bounds. Standing at six foot five with an eighty-inch reach, he clearly was the top American heavyweight prospect; with that distinction came expectations. With those expectations came skeptics. This fact was not lost on Riddick

**Riddick Bowe:** It stung to some degree. I was very young, it was hard to read and hear so much negativity. I won the silver medal. I lost the fight on my feet. I didn't see why everyone felt I was a disgrace. Ferdie Pacheco and folks were giving me no credit. It motivated me. All they can do is talk. In the ring, I determine what the outcome will be.

**Larry Merchant:** There are two reasons that people were low on Riddick coming out of the Olympics, and neither of them had to do with his gold medal loss. Between Tyson, Foreman, and Holyfield, he seemed to lack that something, he seemed to us like a jolly giant, he did not seem all that highly motivated to be the best, that was how he *seemed* to people, and the story about Futch and him is in support of that; he had a reputation for not always being as serious as you have to be, not only to become champ, but to stay there, there was some of that in the air about him. He

**had to convince Futch to be his trainer. Eddie was apprehensive at first because of what he had heard.**

Lionel Butler was not exactly Jack Johnson. He was a fighter with a zero and one record that took the fight on two days' notice. Given those statistics, the general expectations of the fight were low. It was assumed that Riddick would dispatch of him in short order. Michael Buffer gave the two young bulls a tasty introduction, and so began Riddick Bowe's pro career. Usually at the beginning of the fight, there is a feeling-out process in which the two combatants attempt to get a feel of their respective opponent's movement and general timing. This fight did not contain such a process. Both men came out swinging from the opening bell. The fight had a Toughman Contest pace to it. Butler, despite his physical disadvantages, fought valiantly. Even after tasting the canvas. Lionel gave a good account of himself in wake of the knockdown. He charged Riddick and backed him up into the ropes, determined not to show any ill effects of the knockdown. Bowe, amused by the aggression, was content to parry punches and throw some of his own as the round came to a close. Eddie Futch calmly gave his young charge useful instructions between rounds. Riddick rose up from his stool with a quiet confidence that the fight was his. Lionel, to everyone's surprise, including Riddick's, charged out of the corner like he was shot out of a cannon. He engaged Riddick with shocking fury, backing up his bigger opponent with a myriad of body and head punches. It seemed to catch Riddick off guard, given a knockdown had taken place in the previous round. Riddick weathered the storm and began to find his groove. Rolling the punches and slipping the punches, Riddick was cool and collected turning the tide in his favor. As fate would have it, the beginning of the end for Lionel Butler was actually a pair of accidental low blows. The low blows took the steam out of Lionel's courageous aggression. The result was academic from that point on. Riddick began to unload his arsenal on the taxed Butler. He would go on to knock him down twice more in the round, including a tremendous uppercut that wrapped up the proceedings and gave the prospect from Brownsville his first professional victory. The TV announcers, on the call, told the audience that Riddick just wanted to get through his first fight and officially become a professional. He had accomplished that. Even though the fight was brief, Riddick displayed flashes of brilliance. Riddick evenly distributed his punches between the head and the body. He had also withstood some punishment to do it. Riddick Bowe had the ability to fight in close quarters. Riddick, being able to fight on the inside, was mathematically unusual given his reach from shoulders to the fist, not to mention his height.

Riddick had a chance to generate positive fanfare and win over some observers who had dismissed him as a waste of talent. Through his first four professional fights, he had marketed abilities that made him a top prospect on the fistic landscape. The heavyweight division was currently a one-man show. Iron Mike Tyson ruled the heavyweight division at the time. Michael Spinks was the man once seen as the biggest threat to Mike's reign. Had been vanquished by Tyson inside of two minutes the year Riddick took the silver medal. Evander Holyfield, the cruiserweight champion who would emerge as Tyson's most serious contemporary, did not enter that emergence until the turn of the decade. There were no clear-cut challengers or threats to Tyson's throne. Everyone that had been perceived as a threat had been mowed down by Iron Mike. The few that had to the tools to contend with Mike had yet to appraised by the heavyweight gamut. The boxing world was looking for someone who had the balls to contend with the storm that Tyson continually generated in the ring. No one in the universe could have predicted what James "Buster" Douglas would pull off in the New Year. At this point, midway through 1989, the search for the Tyson slayer was all the way live. Riddick, very early in his career, demonstrated he could be that man. The man who could slay the Tyson dragon. When he was right. Despite his unquestioned natural gifts, his tragic flaw according to most boxing insiders (who were not actually inside of camp, mind you) was his lack of mental commitment and acceptable regimen. They believed Riddick lacked the passion to reach peak physical condition. The rumors, while rampant and unconfirmed, did not seem to have much of an effect on the young prospect. Riddick, to his credit, seemed undeterred by all of the dark clouds circling over his head.

**Riddick Bowe: I was not hearin' that bullshit after a while. Just a bunch of white people hatin' on me. With Rock behind me, and Eddie training me, I was focused on the matter at hand. Knocking folks out was my chief concern, not what people thought about me emotionally. Please.**

On July 15, 1989, a twenty-one-year-old Riddick Bowe stepped into the ring for his fifth professional fight. He weighed in at a crisp 225 pounds. To many ringsiders, he appeared to be in true boxing shape. His opponent, Lorenzo Canady, was certainly a tested veteran that was not making his first trip to the rodeo. Lorenzo had been in the ring with the very best heavyweights of the 80s and 90s. He had engaged Mike Tyson, even though that particular tussle only lasted a round. He had been in the ring with respected journeyman Alex Stewart. Lorenzo was also a resident of cruiserweight champion Evander Holyfield's training camp. Lorenzo, despite his stepping stone status, looked to serve as a nice litmus test for Riddick. In the lead up during fight week, Riddick nicknamed himself Batman Bowe. He even sported a classic Caped Crusader T-shirt, much to the amusement of the reporters covering the fight. Riddick, in his own words, credited the new alias as a tribute. He made reference to Tim Burton's indelible full-length feature set to hit theatres shortly after the fight. The fight itself was akin to Batman beating a thug down in the alley. Once the bell rang on fight night, Riddick put everyone at the Marina Hotel and Casino on notice. He brutally executed his camp's game plan at the expense of Lorenzo. He began the fight, establishing his jab. The jab can be as potent as a power punch when utilized correctly. Bowe certainly displayed that type of mastery in the first round of this fight. Riddick's jab was not limited to the head. He was also touching Lorenzo in the solar plexus. Riddick, in the first round, was jabbing to the body consistently. In being versatile with the jab, Riddick was able to set up devastating power shots. Riddick possessed tremendous power. Riddick was landing combinations with power and speed. Once he began sitting on his shots, the result of the fight was only a matter of time and pressure. Riddick even switched to southpaw at one point of the fight, further providing evidence of his unique talents. At the end of the first round, Riddick landed his trademark overhand right, which stumbled Lorenzo and shook up his equilibrium. Bowe pressed the action and landed a right-handed body punch. The body shot was followed by yet another combination that floored Lorenzo as the round drew to a close.

The second round was an indication of the burgeoning technical brilliance of Riddick Bowe. He popped the jab to the head and stomach; he displayed the unusual ability to throw short shots on the inside. He also appeared to have impressive head movement, ducking and slipping almost every punch that was thrown his way. As the round began to reach its conclusion, Riddick again landed two smacking right hands that were followed by a bone-jarring left hook. Riddick punctuated the assault with a straight right hand. The filthy combination was final confirmation. The veteran would quit on his stool fifteen seconds later and give Riddick Bowe his fifth professional victory. Riddick had been undefeated up until this point, but it was this fight that gave the boxing world a glimpse of just how prolific an offensive fighter he could become, under the correct circumstance, at the desired weight. It was a comprehensive reminder to everyone floating doubts. Riddick Bowe could succeed, despite what the people that know everything seemed to project across the board.

Riddick continued his reign of terror in 1989, putting together a September to remember. It was not so much the level of opposition; it was the timetable of activity. The manner in which he dispatched his opponents was robotic. During this whirlwind of a month, he entered the ring three times and left the ring three times with first-round knockouts in tow. In Pensacola, Florida, on September 3, Riddick Bowe stopped Lee Moore in the first round. Two short weeks later, he levied the same devastation upon Anthony Hayes. The ease in which Riddick was running through his opponents was giving him a certain momentum. From a distance his superactive schedule could be seen as too much to ask. Not so, Riddick was producing at such a high level that quick turnarounds were necessary to stay sharp and maintain timing. One round per month is not enough work for a prospect being groomed to be a champion. The most impressive of these three knockouts however came on September 19, four short days after he had been in the ring last.

Riddick Bowe met Earl Lewis on September 19, 1989, at the Veterans Coliseum in Jacksonville, Florida. The fight was broadcast on ESPN too. The bell rung, and so began the combat. Earl Lewis was actually a late replacement and would provide the type of resistance that would make that fact easy to believe. Riddick took his man's measure, which was not much, and pounced with calculating madness. Riddick Bowe saw an opening and took it, landing a six-punch left-right combination that sent Earl down in a human heap. Earl groggily rose to his feet, took the eight count, and reluctantly agreed to continue. Riddick would literally run across the ring and land four punches. The first two would graze, not directly reaching their target. The last two certainly did. Earl was knocked cold by a haymaker left hook; he lost consciousness while still on his feet. The sledgehammer left hook would be followed by a death blow of a straight right hand that sent Earl's head through the bottom ropes and stiffened his lower body. One might have gotten the impression that this combination of punches ended Earl's boxing career. It was not unlike the fourth Rocky installment when Ivan Drago snuffed out Apollo Creed. It was by far the most brutal knockout of Riddick's career and it began to serve notice that a new day in the heavyweight division was possible and maybe even imminent. The fight as a whole took mere 1:25 seconds. The duration of the bout placed the same conundrum on Riddick that the previous two fights did, he needed more work. Even if the fight was not championship level. Trainer Eddie Futch told a beat reporter the reasoning behind such an active schedule.

> "A young heavyweight like Riddick has to stay busy if he is going to continue to progress as a fighter, You can't sit around and wait for big fights to happen. Before Tyson won his title, he was fighting almost every month against all different styles, learning all the time. When he became champion, then he took more time between matches. That's the same blueprint I'd like Riddick to follow."

Riddick took a break of sorts after his September demolition. Some would call four weeks anything but a break. Riddick's next fight would take place on October 19 at the Trump Plaza Hotel and Casino in Atlantic City, New Jersey. Riddick's opponent was a meat-and-potatoes fighter named Mike Acey. Mike Acey, to his credit, had started his career with ten consecutive knockouts. He would not enter the ring in a state of fear. He was not physically or tactically gifted; he lacked the proper head movement to avoid a Mack truck let alone smooth right hands from the Riddick Bowe. Mike had also taken the fight on short notice, which seemed to be a trend for Riddick's early opponents. The fight on paper appeared to be a wash; appearances were correct. In his ninth professional fight, which was broadcasted on USA, Riddick Bowe yet again made short work of a fighter with more professional experience than him. In this fight, Riddick dispensed with some of his weapons, but he utilized others that had not yet really had the chance to prosper. Mike gave as good as he got for the first minute of the round. Mike's arm punches were being caught by Riddick's elbows and gloves; he was throwing and he was coming forward. Riddick, for the most part, was indifferent to the offense being mounted by Mike Acey. There was not a sense of urgency in his approach to mount a counteroffensive. During this first minute of the round, he did land a stiff jab but seemed content to let Mike attack without substantial returns. Riddick's reputation for devastating power must have preceded him at this point. The first feint he threw Mike's way caused Mike to actually turn away from the action and close his eyes. The announcers on the call could not believe it. Riddick had already won the fight mentally before any punches were thrown. Bowe used his speed and athletic disposition to break down Mike rather quickly. He began to potshot Mike, which is unheard of for such a big fighter. It was rather remarkable actually.

Potshotting is a punch in which a fighter will hold his hands at his sides and land quick sharp shots, throwing defensive caution to the wind. This type of punch is a sign that one fighter is physically superior to the other. It also implies that the speed difference is almost comical. Being potshotted is insulting to the fighter that is the victim.

Generally, the next-level athletes of the ring employ and enjoy this specific punch. Roy Jones Jr. and Floyd Mayweather, who are among the most gifted and quickest fighters of all time, use the potshot as their primary offensive weapon respectively. It is hard to find a heavyweight in history that had the physical talent and speed to truly potshot an opponent. Here, Riddick was doing it against a shorter man. After another landed potshot, Riddick landed a straight stiff right that floored the overmatched Acey. Mike seemingly, against his inner judgment, rose at the count of nine. Riddick swarmed all over Mike when the action resumed. Riddick was throwing inaccurate wild shots before calming down and letting the action happen. When he did calm down, he landed a stiff jab that again floored Mike Acey. It really hurt Mike, which is unusual. In boxing, the jab is seen as a secondary punch as opposed to a primary thruster like an uppercut or a hook. The ref told Mike he would "not let him take much more." Mike acknowledged the ref's instructions and bravely stepped forward. Riddick bodied Mike up and promptly landed a powerful uppercut that ended the fight. Any hopes of a letdown by the rising prospect had been dashed. The fight was a wrap. The announcers on the call disputed if Mike actually wanted to fight. That assertion was quasi correct. Upon entering the ring, it was apparent Mike did want to fight. Once he realized what he was up to, his mind-set changed. Nonetheless, Riddick captured his ninth pro victory and appeared ready to take the next step, in terms of his opposition.

# Rock and Eddie

Riddick was unique as it pertained to the infrastructure of his camp. Most fighters have promoters as well as managers. Former middleweight champion Kelly Pavlik is managed by Camron Dunkin but is promoted by Bob Arum. This arrangement is considered conventional by boxing standards. It allows the responsibilities of handling a fighter to be evenly distributed and also ensures fair play to some degree.

A promoter, for example, may have fifty or sixty fighters in his stable. It is difficult for a promoter to focus on one fighter. It is difficult due to the overall responsibility that the promoters' stable demands. Not to mention most promoters such as Don King or Frank Warren care about one person and one person only. That's where the manager comes in. The manager is there to make sure that the fighter does not get overlooked or lost in the shuffle. It could be thought of as a boxing lawyer. Riddick, at the very start of his career, wanted a promoter; he wanted to compete out of someone's stable. This desire, however, fell on deaf ears. He was passed over by many of the big names due to the rumors that constantly surrounded him. This decision would look less than intelligent later. At the time, however, these promoters used intelligent reasoning to go ahead and take a pass.

**Shelly Finkel:** We took a long look at him, and we just didn't see the desire we thought he should have.

Riddick was distraught by his dwindling prospects. For a time he considered enlisting in the armed forces. He revisited this school of thought later in life. Riddick had won the silver medal. But upon his return, it became evident such an achievement would not be parlayed into drooling promoters or Coca-Cola endorsement overtures.

Riddick's saving grace came in the form of a man named Eugene Roderick Newman. Rock Newman was a Howard University graduate, who worked as a guidance counselor at the same university. Rock got his start in the boxing business as an assistant for the famous Butch Lewis. Although Riddick was not the first fighter that Rock managed (he managed Dwight Muhammad Qawi), he certainly was the first big-time prospect that Rock attempted to handle.

Rock was the only person in boxing that truly believed that Riddick could be cultivated into a heavyweight champion. To Rock's credit, he truly went out on a limb for Riddick. Rock made a personal and financial investment into Riddick, essentially going all in. He signed Riddick to a managerial contract that included a signing bonus. Access to a car sweetened the deal for the starving prospect from Brownsville. It was not as if Rock Newman was Daddy Warbucks or a top-level executive at J. P. Morgan. He invested a good amount of his wealth into the project. Rock used the capital from mortgaging his own home to underwrite Riddick's contract and subsequent expenses. Rock also agreed to pay the purses of all of Riddick's opponents until the big money started rolling in. Rock Newman, in retrospect, was a true visionary, if only he had gone into the stock market. Rock would take one-third of all of Riddick's boxing revenue, but even that would not kick in until Riddick started making acceptable purses. Not a bad deal for a kid from the hood that no one had high expectations of. Rock, in so many words, *was* Riddick's promoter but was smart enough not to assume that title.

Rock Newman is as responsible for the rise of Riddick Bowe as anyone. Anybody that says different either has a personal problem with Rock Newman or is selling something. Rock Newman made another move that was crucial to Riddick's development. He recruited the best possible trainer that Riddick could have had. After a look around, he settled on Eddie Futch.

Eddie Futch is a cornerstone of boxing history. Eddie Futch's boxing pedigree was immaculate. Eddie Futch had trained heavyweight legends such as Joe Frazier, Larry Holmes, and Ken Norton. A boxer himself, Eddie Futch had enjoyed a stellar amateur career in his hometown of Detroit, Michigan. Training in the same gym as Joe Louis, Futch won a Golden Gloves lightweight championship. He was set to turn pro before revelation of a heart murmur stalled his plans. Eddie Futch went on to become one of the great trainers in history.

By the time Riddick Bowe came along, Eddie was an old man "who didn't not have much time to waste." The boxing community is a small empire, and Eddie Futch was well aware of the Riddick Bowe rumors. Rock Newman made contact with Eddie about the possibility of working with Riddick. The Hall of Fame trainer at first was not keen on the prospects of the project.

**Eddie Futch:** **I questioned his desire, I'd heard he was lazy, didn't have much heart or discipline. I was seventy-eight then, and I told Rock Newman (Bowe's manager) that I didn't have enough time left to waste it on someone like that.**

Rock Newman aggressively recruited Eddie. Even when it became apparent that Futch was not very open to training a fighter who had fostered a reputation for maximum talent but minimal production. There were also questions about Riddick Bowe's work ethic. Eddie, after lengthy discussion with Rock, agreed to meet Bowe and get a feel of him personally. This encounter was not your run-of-the-mill meeting in a nice restaurant. This was Bowe reporting to Las Vegas and going right to work. Eddie wanted to throw Bowe right in the fire, see what type of reaction it would precipitate. The day after Riddick arrived, in the wee hours of morning, Riddick Bowe was tested. Eddie Futch's mind was the control group.

**Richard Steele:** **Eddie Futch was an all-time great trainer. He was my trainer when I was a boxer. I met Eddie in 1967. My uncle was the lightweight champion of California. He and Eddie fought at the same time. When I got out of the marine corps, my uncle persuaded Eddie to take me on. I, along with Ken Norton Sr., went straight from the service to Eddie Futch's care. I learned so much from him, and I knew he made Bowe even more dangerous than he already was. Eddie could look at any fighter and figure out how to beat him. He would always tell his fighters, "You fight the first round, I will do the rest." Riddick Bowe was very talented, but it was Eddie Futch who put him over the top. The day Riddick flew into Vegas to meet Eddie was something else.**

Eddie told Bowe he wanted him up and doing his roadwork at five in the morning. He wanted to see how committed Riddick was. Riddick sure enough got up on time and did his roadwork. While he was in the midst of his workout, he was sandbagged by Eddie. Eddie had gotten up early to check whether or not Riddick followed instructions. That was the icebreaker. Eddie, like everyone else, had heard he was lazy and did not work hard. Eddie was in his late seventies and did not want to waste time with someone who didn't have the drive. That morning was important to their relationship. Eddie knew Riddick was talented but needed more to take him on. All Riddick needed was good coaching. In the amateurs, you don't really have your own trainer. A lot of bad habits go uncorrected. Those days were over for Riddick. Eddie made all the difference in the world.

After some initial trepidation, Eddie agreed to take Bowe on as his last client. Being the last fighter that Eddie Futch ever trained is an immeasurable honor in the boxing community. Eddie Futch was one of the most celebrated boxing trainers of his time or any time really. From sparring with Joe Louis to helping Joe Frazier upset Muhammad Ali, Eddie was a true national treasure. Bowe and Eddie's relationship was much more than a trainer-fighter partnership. There was an immediate emotional bond. Thell Torrence was a firsthand observer of the dynamics of the two.

**Thell Torrence:** Eddie and Riddick would clash heads. Eddie was of the thinking that he wanted things done his way, and he wanted them done right now. Sometimes this would be hard for Riddick to deal with. It would take me stepping in to some to get Riddick to buy in, but he always would end up doing what Eddie asked of him. Riddick respected Eddie deeply, even loved him. Eddie laid down the ground rules from the start. Eddie had a way of doing things in camp.

**Riddick would have trouble with this because he was kind of a joker; he was not the most serious guy in the world, you know what I mean? Eddie on the other hand was very serious. It could only be compared to father-son relationship.**

Rock Newman had something to prove. He had been a lackey for Butch Lewis. He was eager to prove that he could build a champion of his own. Rock also wanted to prove that he was smarter than everyone else. All the major promoters had passed on Riddick Bowe. Rock Newman was determined prove all of them wrong. Riddick and Rock's agendas were intertwined. Both of them had something to prove to the boxing world, and they set about doing it together. Believing in each other, even if no one else did at the time

## 4

# Climbing the Ladder

Riddick would close out 1989 in the usual exciting fashion. On December 14, he tangled with pedestrian heavyweight Charles "White Lightning" Woolard. The fight took place in St. Joseph, Missouri. This fight came just over three weeks after Riddick Bowe's last trip to the ring. Riddick had also shed six pounds since his last tour of duty, which implied consistent work in the gym since the last engagement. Charles Woolard had to this point compiled a record of 13–2. He was a tall gangly heavyweight but seemed less dangerous all the same. During the introductions, there was a curious occurrence. The announcer introduced Charles Woolard. Before introducing Bowe, the announcer presented Eddie Futch to the crowd; Futch's introduction elicited a rousing ovation. It seemed strange given the fact that this side introduction could have taken place before the fighters were introduced, or after. The fact that he was the first person in Riddick's corner to be introduced was funny to say the least. The other interesting component of the introductions, that perhaps explained the former, was the identity of the announcer. The man originally assigned to the prefight introductions had been a victim of snowy conditions. As a result, Rock Newman himself presided over the introductions. Rock did an effective job communicating the proceedings to those in attendance. At this point in his career, Riddick's nickname had been changed from Batman Bowe to Iceman Bowe. The Iceman was greeted warmly by the crowd, and so began the action.

Riddick Bowe, in this particular fight, was beginning to show an understanding of how to conduct business in the ring. He had a man in front of him that did not have much to offer. Riddick still gave him the proper respect and let his offense come. For the first minute of the opening round, Riddick popped his jab and showed lateral movement. He also dropped in a potshot here and there. As the round began to come to its conclusion, the Iceman went on to attack. With sudden violence that had become his trademark, he landed two cracking overhand rights. The combination moved Charles to hold on for dear life. Riddick broke the hold and landed two more nasty right hands as the first round came to a close. Charles did not seem fully recovered at the start of the second round, actually wobbling on his feet as he rose out of his stool. The second round started like the first. Riddick was looking to set up the conclusion of the fight with his punishing jab. Charles, to his credit, fought with a sense of urgency, throwing wild winging shots. The punches hit nothing but air, and Riddick was ducking and slipping with ease. Bowe began to fight like young Cassius Clay. Dancing on his feet, throwing right hand leads, keeping his hands at his sides. Having the white trunks with black trim did not hurt either. It was a beautiful display of the sweet science. The conclusion of the fight also looked like something out of the past. The Iceman landed a brutal jab–right hand combination that sent Charles crashing to the floor, flat on his back. Charles got up and went on the offensive. Riddick absorbed all the arm punches and bided his time. Bowe chased Charles into the ropes and landed two monster body shots that floored Charles yet again. Charles was in agony as he rose to his feet, nose bloodied. He stepped forward only to be met with another body shot. Charles sank to the canvas, violating the three knockdown rules, handing Riddick another easy TKO victory. Charles was in absolute distress as he attempted to collect himself. Gil Clancy, who was the call, actually said something positive about Riddick Bowe in the wake of the knockout.

"There is really not much more a Riddick Bowe could do, he really looked good."

Gil was the same guy that had bashed Riddick early in his career. Riddick has his victory moved to 13–0. At this point, it seemed to many that Riddick had displayed enough skills to go after the next tier of heavyweight competition, although it would be a year or so before that would come to pass.

Over the next year and half, Riddick Bowe continued to make his presence known in the heavyweight ranks. Although the level of his opposition would be calibrated to a low setting, the Riddick Bowe freight train showed no signs of slowing down or letting up. In four of his next five fights, he would register knockouts. The only fighter who would make it to the final bell during that stretch would be respected veteran Pinklon Thomas. Don't get it twisted. Pinklon Thomas was never a truly relevant heavyweight champion, but he had been an alphabet titleholder and shared the ring with the great heavyweights of his day. The fact that he was the lone man to survive a full eight rounds was not an indictment on Riddick but more so of a proof that Pinklon was still somewhat viable, even at that late stage of his career.

# 5

# Smokin'

Riddick Bowe's next opponent was a boxer that defined the word *journeyman* over the course of his career. Smokin' Bert Cooper fought everyone there was to fight during a heavyweight campaign that spanned two decades. He had retained the famous nickname Smokin' as a tribute to his trainer Smokin' Joe Frazier. Bert was a short stocky fighter. Bert Cooper harbored a sneaky right hand and a hood mentality. Even though Riddick Bowe would be the much bigger man, it was generally understood that Bert was not going to take no for an answer. Bert Cooper was not to be underestimated. Bert also had recently designated himself as nothing to sneeze at, taking Olympian Ray Mercer to the limit in his last trip to the ring. Ray Mercer had competed in the same Olympics as Riddick Bowe and, like Riddick, was an undefeated American prospect. Riddick Bowe, in fighting Bert Cooper, had an indirect opportunity to make a statement to his critics, and Ray Mercer as well.

The fight took place at the Mirage Hotel and Casino on October 25, 1990. Riddick weighed in at 230 pounds while Cooper would weigh in at 208 pounds. Riddick Bowe's purse amounted to $40,000 for the fight. Bowe's official weight caused a little bit of a controversy. Largely due to the fact that Eddie Futch had actually been recovering from hip surgery during training camp. Bowe appearing slightly overweight was seen as a by-product of that absence. Eddie, being the cagey veteran that he was, managed to work the fight despite his documented health issues. Bowe, standing six foot five, would have a marked size advantage over Cooper. Bert Cooper stood a mere five foot eleven. The lighting rod known as Richard Steele was third man in the ring. The fight started before it began. The fighters approached the center of the ring and listened to the traditional prefight instructions from Richard. Usually at the end of the instructions, the fighters are expected to touch gloves as a gesture of sportsmanship. It is seen as an act of goodwill before the two fighters engage in mortal combat. Bert Cooper, for whatever reason, saw the need to lightly punch Bowe. Riddick smiled through his mouth guard and attempted to head back to his corner. For whatever reason, Richard Steele seems to be involved in strange occurences in the ring that is well documented, just ask Meldrick Taylor or Razor Ruddock. Richard decided to bring both men back to the center of the ring to try it again. Riddick Bowe, as the world was beginning to find out, was not a soft individual. Riddick responded in kind, jabbing Bert in the ribs when they reconvened in the middle of the ring. This was followed by a long stare down; Richard Steele finally realized that getting to the two men to display sportsmanship was simply not going to happen. They returned to their corners and waited for the opening bell

**Richard Steele: There was a lot of tension during those prefight instructions. I think it was more Bert then Bowe; they didn't seem to like each other. I wanted them to stop acting like children and just touch gloves, but they didn't want to.**

The fight began with Cooper, and his Napoleon complex, taking the fight right to Bowe. Cooper was a heavy-handed puncher. He lived up to that reputation by landing a solid left hook ten seconds into the fight. Bert Cooper was well aware of the reach advantage that Bowe enjoyed. Cooper attempted to counteract the reach disparity by swarming Riddick Bowe. Bert attempted to work inside that reach. Riddick, at the onset, appeared to be content catching punches and taking the measure of his man. He did not appear to be too concerned with the sneaky punching power of Bert Cooper. Cooper, to his credit, simply did not allow Riddick to work at a preferred distance in the first round. He was mauling Riddick, not allowing him to use his superior reach. Cooper won the first round due to the lack of purchase that Riddick was able to create.

Eddie Futch, still not 100 percent well due to surgery, gave Riddick proper instructions between rounds. Eddie sat on a stool set up on the floor of the arena, next to the corner. He instructed Bowe to create distance with his jab and use his uppercut. Riddick took the advice and applied it. Popping his jab, Bowe created some space at the very beginning of the second round. Once Bowe had the created the proper distance, he began to open up, throwing combinations, really placing Bert on the defensive for the first time in the fight. In the last minute of the round, Riddick timed an incoming Cooper with a picture-perfect right hand that laid waste to Cooper's senses. Bowe landed another clean right hand with Bert's defenses disabled. The second right hand set Bert down on his backside. Bert rose to his feet as the round came to a close but would be sent back to the canvas after another barrage by Bowe. Richard Steele, who had a history of making bad stoppages, made the right call in this particular situation, calling the fight at the conclusion of the second round. Riddick Bowe had taken heat for his weight and focus prior to the fight. He had now made a statement to the boxing world, easily dispatching of a relatively live heavyweight in Bert Cooper. The victory was impressive, no doubt about it, given the manner in which he went about his business. Riddick returned to the ring one more time in 1990, knocking out Tony Morrison (not Tommy) in one round on December 14.

It had been a tremendous year for Riddick Bowe. He had made the tricky transition from being a prospect with buzz to a rising contender with clout. The eight victories that Riddick furnished in 1990 all showed different traits that made it clear he could one day be heavyweight champion. As 1990 drew to a close, Riddick Bowe was 20–0. He seemed destined for the next level of competition and purses. He really had no choice. He had proven he was a viable heavyweight; it was now time to be truly tested. An undefeated record and fifty cents gets you a bus ticket from most boxing insiders. When you have the whispers floating about you that Riddick did, the bar is very high. It's interesting that was the way of things. In modern times for example, Alfredo Angulo was 15–0 when he was handed an HBO contract and an interim title belt. Mike Tyson had set the bar so high at the time, it was near impossible to impress without looking like the next Clubber Lang. The good news for Riddick, however, was that he had made it through the first leg of his professional career unscathed and was now ready to take the next step. Riddick would be entering a new territory in the New Year. A territory where first-round knockouts and part-time plumbers would be hard to come by. He was entering a phase of his career where he would have to prepare and truly put the work in. He would also have to respect his opponents. The latter would prove to be a little trickier than it seemed.

# 6

# Biggs

Riddick Bowe took a step up in class when he engaged former Olympic gold medalist Tyrell Biggs. Tyrell had been Riddick Bowe's sparring partner during Riddick's time in Evander Holyfield's camp. Biggs, unlike Bowe, was red hot after participating in the Olympic Games. After taking a gold medal at the LA Olympics in 1984, Tyrell burst onto the boxing scene with considerable vengeance, winning his first fifteen fights. The winning streak seemed to justify the gold medal hype. The streak landed him a fight with Iron Mike Tyson. It seemed to some like flawed career advice at the time, that is not meant as disrespect to Shelly Finkel. Tyrell had only fought fifteen pro fights. Biggs challenged for the undisputed heavyweight championship against the seemingly unbeatable Mike Tyson. Tyrell was knocked out in seven rounds but gave a good account of himself in the process. Tyrell went on to lose three straight fights, including the Tyson fight, before rebounding to win four in row prior to meeting Bowe. Tyrell Biggs was a desperate man. He viewed Bowe as a public relations vessel to bigger fights and greener pastures. That fact made this a dangerous fight for Riddick and demanded sharp focus. The fight was set for March 2, 1991. The fight was broadcast on ABC's *Wide World of Sports*. This was back in the days when synergy existed between boxing and network television. The telecast did a great job of presenting the two Americans to the viewing public. Based on the styles, the fight looked to be physical. The numbers were hard to ignore. Riddick, standing six foot five, having an arm reach of eighty-one inches, stood as an imposing heavyweight. Tyrell was no physical slouch either; standing six foot five himself he appeared to be Riddick's physical equal. As far as inches go, Tyrell Biggs held complete parity with Riddick Bowe. Riddick retained the advantage in the power department. The crossroads fight took place at the Harrah's Hotel and Casino in Atlantic City. Both men weighed in at 225 pounds. That was very telling. If you look at their respective weight fluctuations over the years, that would tell anyone that both these men realized the importance of this fight and put the work into win it.

Given the physical disposition of both men, one could expect caution being thrown to the wind. The two combatants would not disappoint. Riddick seemed to have a sense of urgency at the onset of the bout. That or he simply viewed Tyrell as another one of his early-knockout victims. Riddick stepped toward Tyrell, parried a couple punches, and then landed a humongous right hand, sending Tyrell into a moonwalk back to the distant corner. Riddick proceeded to pursue and swarm Tyrell with tumultuous activity less than forty-five seconds into the fight. Tyrell, to his credit, would not bite the dust that easily. Riddick, in the midst of an all-out assault, was not really worried about punches coming back at him. Tyrell took advantage of this, landing a solid left hook that blunted Riddick's forward progress; the hook let the young lion know this fight would be no easy way out. The left hook most likely was Riddick's introduction to the next level of heavyweight competition. After absorbing the left hook, he knew he had entered a realm where getting knocked out was possible if he did not properly defend himself. In retrospect, it was a big moment in Riddick's career. The first round of the fight was not unlike Hagler versus Hearns; less explosive of course, both men were throwing fight-ending shots. It was true unedited violence. Tyrell would notice that his nose was bleeding sixty seconds into the fight. Biggs was also doing something that appeared to bother Riddick. It would continue to bother Riddick for much of the fight. Tyrell was utilizing the jab in all aspects. Tyrell was jabbing to the head and body, making it difficult for Riddick to truly time him. Tyrell also had the physical gift to effectively employ the jab, given his parity with the reach. Biggs closed out the first round in style, outlanding Bowe with a combination of jabs and left hooks, really getting to him. Riddick Bowe was in the ring with a well-seasoned boxing technician.

In between rounds, Eddie Futch reminded Riddick that Tyrell, after being cracked with the right hand, would now be looking for it. He implored Riddick to use his jab to set up the right. The second round began much the way the first one ended. Tyrell again effectively used the jab to keep Riddick at bay. Tyrell also continued to cut the left hook loose when Riddick breached the outer perimeter. It was a decent strategy; it did not, however, preclude Riddick from landing some meaningful punches. This confluence of punches began to take its toll on Tyrell's face. Tyrell's eyes were beginning to close. Towards the end of the second round, Riddick got cute and posed in front of Tyrell. Tyrell responded by landing a jarring left hook that wobbled Bowe into the ropes; the punch put Riddick on the defensive for the first time in his career. Riddick motioned Tyrell to come on in and throw some more shots. It was clear that Tyrell had gotten to him for the second time in the fight.

In the fourth round, Riddick began to see the fruits of his efforts. Tyrell developed a cut over his left eye. Tyrell had a history being cut over that very same eye. Riddick would continue the tradition courtesy of some well-placed right hands. This turn of events seemed to be the turning point of the fight. Tyrell, who had seemed in control, now appeared in trouble. Biggs would have more good moments as the fight wore on, even stunning Bowe in the sixth round with a good one-two combination. His body language, however, indicated that he was a spent force; it was only a matter of time before Riddick got to him. Tyrell was clearly on his downhill in the eighth round as Riddick battered him. Tyrell finally succumbed to the pressure. After taking an overhand right that sent him crumbling to the canvas, Tyrell had given everything he had. He still managed to get up and continue the fight. Riddick greeted Tyrell with a savage right hand that brought a commission member onto the ring apron to call the fight. Riddick had registered his twenty-second victory at forty-two seconds of the eighth round. It was a good tough test for the young fighter. Riddick passed the test with good marks. Tyrell Biggs certainly was not the cream of heavyweight crop, but he had provided young Riddick Bowe with an idea of what it would take to exceed at the highest level. Tyrell Biggs did win in one respect though. Some boxing insiders have said that Tyrell laid the original blueprint for defeating Riddick Bowe. If you can jab Riddick Bowe, you can beat him.

The next opponent for Riddick Bowe was rugged journeyman Tony Tubbs. Tony Tubbs was more than a perennial contender. He was a former heavyweight champion, and his two losses came at the hands of former world champions. He was well built and slick. The fight had become an unofficial showcase for Riddick Bowe because of the events of the previous night. Twenty-four hours before Riddick stepped in the ring to take on Tubbs, George Foreman and Evander Holyfield had staged one of the more exciting heavyweight fights in recent years. George had fallen to Evander but, in defeat, proved that Evander Holyfield had his limits when it came to fighting bigger men. In the wake of Evander's victory, the boxing world was eager for a fresh young heavyweight that could push Evander down the stretch of a fight. Riddick Bowe, according to some observers, could be that heavyweight. The burden of proof was on Riddick Bowe to not only win but look impressive doing so. He was twenty-three years old, and it seemed like his title shot was getting closer and closer. Rock Newman could not have picked a tougher opponent to showcase his fighter's offensive abilities. Tony Tubbs did not possess cracking power. He was a well-schooled veteran with a good jab and a decent shoulder roll to boot. Not the type of fighter that normally cooperates with a showcase fight.

Riddick Bowe entered the toughest fight of his career unbeknownst to him. Tony Tubbs started the fight a little tentative, not wanting to engage the hungry young challenger. Riddick took advantage of this apprehension, badly hurting Tubbs in the first round and proceeding to go for the quick knockout. Tubbs weathered the storm and made it out of the first round, which was a credit to him; many of Riddick Bowes early opponents did not do this much. Riddick fought a different fight. He was not double jabbing and seemed content to let Tubbs move about the ring without resistance. Tony Tubbs fought a decent technical fight, hooking off his jab and giving Riddick some things to think about as the fight went on. Riddick was never hurt by Tony's counter punching, he was, however, getting hit a little more often than Rock Newman or Eddie Futch would have liked. The fight was meant to be a showcase; it quickly became a competition. As the overweight Tony Tucker began to run out of gas, he became content to lie on the ropes, fighting slickly on the inside when he was pressed. It became even more difficult for Riddick to land clean effective blows. Riddick was winning the fight based on punch output. He was losing in the court of public opinion. The energy he was expending against a seemingly overmatched opponent was not winning him votes in the media. Tubbs rallied towards the end of the fight, putting the icing on Riddick Bowe's average performance. Riddick Bowe won the fight on all three score cards, but it was much closer than anyone though possible going into the fight. None of the scorecards featured a margin larger than three rounds.

Riddick Bowe won the battle but lost the public relations war. The performance caused many to surmise that Riddick was not ready for the big show despite the fact that Tony Tubbs boasted a world-class resume. Riddick Bowe was not a gold medalist, but he was being held to a gold medal standard. It seemed unfair to the rising contender, but that's the nature of a boxing beast. The Tony Tubbs fight was seen as a wake-up call to Riddick and his handlers. Riddick Bowe was determined to not let this latest indictment define his current status. He had won the fight, but it was clear that there was a lot of work to do before he was truly ready to take a shot at the heavyweight title.

Riddick's next fight took place on June 28 at the Mirage Hotel and Casino. The fight that took place as the sun was setting behind the Nevada mountains. It was a strange day to be fighting. The wind was gusting up to thirty miles an hour while the temperature was scorching at ninety degrees. Bowe, clearly in the midst of a revelation (many thanks to Tony Tubbs), weighed in at 226 pounds. Marin, a native Puerto Rican, stood six foot four and weighed in at 230 pounds. Marin sported an impressive 17–1 record; fourteen of those victories came by knockout. "The Classy" Jimmy Lennon Jr. presided over the introductions. After Jimmy did his thing, veteran official Carlos Padilla gave the prefight instructions. For whatever reason, neither man was open to giving an inch. They simply stared at each other, refusing to touch gloves. The good news for fight fans in attendance was that Marin had come to compete by all appearances; the bad news is that he would now have to prove it. Riddick Bowe started the fight, establishing his vaunted jab and creating a distance early, something he failed to do in the Tony Tubbs fight. His jab was snapping Marin's head back, gaining Riddick a lot of respect in the early going. Riddick suddenly landed a one-two combination. The combination took the steam out of Marin very early in the first round. Riddick continued to punish Marin with his jab as the round wore on. Riddkick seemingly outclassed his opponent, serving notice that it would be a short night at the office. The second round was more of the same. Riddick was beating Marin up with his jab, looking to set up the right hand. Riddick used the jab to unleash a nasty uppercut that snapped Marin's head up in the air. Marin's head snapping back allowed Riddick to land four more punches. Marin attempted to clinch in order to stem the tide, but the end was near. Riddick broke the clinch and landed a clubbing overhand right followed by another uppercut that sent Marin to the floor. Marin sat there, pondered getting up, and then thought better of it as he was counted out at

1:16 of the first round.

**Riddick Bowe:** Those early years were so much fun. I was getting knockouts and proving everyone wrong. I was moving up fast and getting respect. Some people like Larry Merchant and Ferdie Pacheco would still doubt me publicly, but it was getting to a point where even those dudes had to recognize my talent.

Ferdie Pacheco was Ali's fight doctor. He is renowned in the sport for his passion and knowledge. His career in television eclipsed his career in boxing. Ferdie Pacheco was highly respected by the viewing public. He was an astute and colorful analyst. His opinions were considered to have merit and base. He covered boxing at the 1988 Olympics for the US TV carrier. During that time, he spent a lot of time with Riddick and took a disliking to Riddick's constant Ali impersonations. When he derided Riddick Bowe following the 1988 Olympics, he infected a lot of inquiring minds. Many assumed his views, and it affected Riddick Bowe's career. Ferdie was not the only source of the bad buzz, but he certainly did his part. As luck would have it, Ferdie was on the call for King Vision (Don King production's pay-per-view carrier) that afternoon. The man who bashed Riddick Bowe when was a young heavyweight hopeful was singing a different tune on this day. He was, instead, complimenting Riddick throughout the fight for his offensive skill set. Even Riddick's loudest critics were beginning to see what everyone else could. Riddick Bowe was turning a corner, and his time was drawing near. Dealing with a Ferdie Pacheco or a Skip Bayless is an evil that every top athlete must deal with. Critics will always be out there.

**Riddick Bowe:** Fuck 'em. Everyone that doubted me or told me I would never be good enough. The writers and reporters, the boxing people that talked greasy about me. All of of them. I was doing my thing.

# The Express

Bowe was beginning to ease into the transition of being a major contender; this stage would see him rise to marvelous heights in the heavyweight division. He had successfully waded his way through the club fighter stage. Riddick Bowe was knee-deep in the gatekeeper phase. The term gatekeeper in boxing is designated for fighters who no longer fight at a world-class level. Fighters that still have enough juice to provide a young prospect a proper appraisal to inquiring boxing minds. Someone like Joel Julio or an Edison Miranda are prime examples of gatekeepers in the game of boxing. This stage is crucial to selling the fighter to networks and the public. With the rare exception of Amir Khan, most top-flight talent enters and exits this stage unblemished. Riddick had the chance to separate himself from pedestrian heavyweights. He sought to make a push towards the Mt. Olympus section of the division.

Riddick Bowe continued upon his heavyweight conquest in the fall of 1991. His newest victim was a fighter by the name of Bruce Seldon. The "Atlantic City Express" was a very respectable heavyweight at the time, having won his first eighteen fights before knocking himself out at the hands of Oliver McCall. Bruce was not a stellar amateur, having only fought twenty-five fights before turning pro. He was rough and tough and fighting at home. Bruce needed a marquee win to atone for his setback in the McCall fight. He had been dropped out of the top fifteen by most of the sanctioning bodies and was in danger of losing his up-and-comer status. This made him someone to be reckoned with. At least in theory anyway. Riddick came into the fight realizing that protection of his rising position was paramount. Riddick Bowe was ranked in the top ten by all four sanctioning bodies. He was closing in on a title shot. Riddick Bowe weighed in at 225 pounds. From all accounts, he was focused on the matter at hand. Bruce Seldon, in all his glory, informed reporters before the fight that he planned to pressure the bigger and stronger Bowe. It seemed like strategic disaster and was met with obvious skepticism.

The fight took place September 9 at Convention Hall on the Boardwalk of Atlantic City. The fight headlined the entire card, a sign that Riddick Bowe's star was rising in the boxing world.

As Michael Buffer went about the introductions, Bruce Seldon gave every indication that a war was at hand. Bruce Seldon could sell one hell of a wolf ticket. Riddick Bowe was confident yet introverted during these very same introductions, ready to make another statement to the doubters that were still alive and well. Bruce started the fight keeping his word. He unloaded power shots on the bigger man, truly going for broke, not worrying that much about defense. It was wild pressure, but it was pressure nonetheless. Bruce was dispensing some serious heat to Riddick's body. The punches were not landing, but Bruce was letting Riddick know that he was here to fight. Riddick had the ability to remain calm in the ring; the pace of the action was not overwhelming him. He seemed indifferent to the pressure. Riddick was not going to let Bruce feel like he had a chance to actually win the fight. When a fighter comes out with a head of steam the way Bruce did, there's a lull in the tide. The great fighters over the course of boxing history have had a knack for shooting that gap. Riddick did just that, landing a stiff jab followed by a freight-train right hand. The punch was of such speed and power, it took Bruce three seconds to realize he had been caught. Bruce Seldon crashed to the canvas. Bruce's body language on the canvas suggested that the fight was over. Then suddenly at the count of eight, Bruce exploded up from the canvas and jumped full force into the air. It was one of the strangest moments in recent boxing memory. Riddick Bowe would find out later in life; the weird and unexplained would always follow him in the ring, like flies to horseshit. After Bruce beat the count, he stepped right back into the pocket with Bowe, throwing power shots. Riddick Bowe landed a crushing blow to the body that froze Seldon. Bowe then came back with a left hook to the jaw that destabilized Seldon. Bruce would not beat the count. Riddick scored the knockout at 1:13 of the first round. This victory was not against a club fighter or a weekday window washer. It had come to a man with one fight that removed him from the top ten. The victory was a huge stepping stone; the fight solidified Riddick's position as a top ten heavyweight. Rock Newman, in wake of the knockout, ran into the ring and sprinted toward the corner that Bruce Seldon had occupied during the fight. He pointed into the crowd and began to shout at an onlooker who was observing with some interest. Rock waved his arms, inviting the onlooker to fight Riddick next. The interested observer was Ray Mercer. Ray Mercer was a Riddick Bowe contemporary in every sense of the word. He had come out of the same Olympic tournament, he was undefeated, and he was climbing the heavyweight ranks. A clash between Riddick Bowe and Ray Mercer seemed like a matter of time; this was not lost on Rock Newman. He almost seemed to be telling Ray Mercer that the worst thing in the world for his career at this point was a fight with Riddick Bowe. After such an awesome performance, it was clear why Ray's handlers did not chase the fight in the months or years that followed. Ray Mercer had come to the fight to scout Riddick for himself. Upon scouting, Ray Mercer was not spotted at a Riddick Bowe fight for quite awhile thereafter. The fans in attendance noticed the dynamics between Riddick and Ray. The crowd began to chant Ray's name, goading him to come in the ring. Rock Newman circled the ring with a Cheshire cat grin, loudly telling Riddick he was going to be the next heavyweight champion of the world. Based on the level of that night's production, it would have been quite difficult to refute Rocks assertions. Riddick appeared headed for the big time. Bowe was truly hitting his stride as one of the most dangerous heavyweights in the world.

Riddick Bowe and his handlers were now under the ever-watchful eyes of the boxing world. Gone were the days in which Riddick could be dismissed as cannon fodder. Gone were the days where the doubts about his desire to win could be given solvent merit. Riddick Bowe was primed for boxing success. He was in the driver's seat to become boxing's next big superstar. It had been a long road to make it to this point, and he had not even arrived at the ultimate destination. The purses and the stages were getting a little bigger. The key at this stage of the journey was to stay the course, to parlay this latest progression into a dream he had been chasing for over a decade. Riddick's next fistic assignment would come in the form of heavyweight Elijah Tillary. Any boxing scribe or soothsayer could not have predicted the events that would follow.

# 8

# The Karate Kid

Elijah Tillary was a decent heavyweight that packed serviceable punching power. He was a product of the Staten Island, New York. He certainly would not be intimidated come fight night. Elijah was built like an action figure. He had physical gifts but lacked boxing IQ. Before the fight actually came off, there was nothing to suggest that this particular opponent would be anything special, or much of a departure from the foes that Bowe had blown away over the course of his four-year career. The fight was held at the former Washington DC convention center. The convention center has since moved down the street, but this fight was held in the original building before the city of Washington DC constructed the new one. The fight took place on October 29, 1991. Tillary, before the fight, would do everything he could to unsettle Riddick. Everything from threatening him and his family to actually blowing a kiss at Riddick before the opening bell. To those in Riddick's camp, Tillary had breached the boundary of gamesmanship and seemed headed towards the socially awkward territory. There were some indications that they might be dealing with a potentially explosive situation. The fight began as many of Riddick's fight had begun. He was bum-rushed by the smaller man. Many of Riddick's opponents were so overcome with his size that they felt the only way to attack Bowe was to go right at him. The problem with that logic was Bowe was not an unintelligent plodding giant. He had tremendous boxing skills and was ring savvy. Elijah went on the attack, attempting to back Bowe up with hooks and stiff jabs. Bowe simply let the fight evolve on its own, attempting to get Elijah's timing. Bowe began his own offensive, jabbing to the body, which always produced positive returns when done correctly. Elijah became aware of the jab to the body; at that very moment, Bowe caught him with an overhand right that wobbled Elijah into the ropes. Bowe pursued Elijah with controlled rage, unleashing all kinds of firepower. Tillery, realizing the gravity of his situation, held on for dear life and attempted to weather the storm. Tillery ran for the next minute of the round, trying to avoid the crushing blows that were coming his way from all angles. Bowe at this point in his career knew he had to finish his man when he had him hurt. Tillery was a journeyman fighter in every sense of the word. He did a masterful job of clinching and grappling, determined not to give Bowe a chance to land a clean shot that would end the fight. The referee was not impressed with the constant clinching. The referee warned Tillery that he would deduct a point if Elijah did not show some type of lust for combat. Following the warning, Bowe stalked Elijah and cornered him, landing vicious body shots. He punctuated his body attack with a right hand upstairs that sent Elijah to the canvas. Elijah took the 8-count and agreed to resume the action. Subsequently, Bowe went right back on the attack as the round drew to a close.

A logistical hiccup would come next. The round ended officially according to the timekeeper. After the timekeeper rang his bell, the round continued. What would follow is a moment that will forever live in the annals of all-time weird. When the ref signaled that the round was over, Elijah did not return to his corner; he actually blew a kiss at Riddick, much to the shock of those ringside and, to some degree, Riddick himself. Bowe, not thinking clearly, reacted with some anger, shooting a left jab at Tillery's puckered lips. Elijah responded by attempting to kick Riddick three times. He kicked him twice and then a third time as he retreated into the ropes. There is a belief amongst observers that Elijah knew he had no chance to win; in the face of utter destruction, he regressed to his ghetto roots. It's difficult to get in the ring and fight a better man. It is that much more difficult to hide who you are and where you are from. Bowe was angered by the lack of sportsmanship by Tillery. He chased him into the ropes, throwing back alley right hands, no longer concerned with winning the fight.

**Riddick Bowe:** That shit pissed me off. He blew that kiss at me, dog, and I lost it. He had also blown a kiss at me during the prefight instructions. I didn't even care of I won the fight at that point. Who does that? He was one of the strangest people I have ever met in my life. He is lucky I didn't get to him. I remember Rock Newman jumping up on the mat and grab-

**bing Tillery. At that point, some of Tillery's people grabbed Rock and dragged him down to the floor. Rock still had his arms around the dude's neck and that's why they went over the ropes. People think Rock pulled Tillery over the ropes. That's not true, *he* was pulled to the floor and took Tillery with him**

At this point, the scene became chaotic. The visibly concerned Rock Newman stepped onto the ring apron and grabbed Elijah by the neck. Rock was then grabbed by Tillery's handlers and dragged to the floor with Tillery as Riddick was bashing Elijah's face in. Elijah, once he hit the floor, was corralled by police on the scene and escorted back into the ring. He was subsequently disqualified. As the two camps waited in the ring for the final decision to be announced, the two sides jawed back and forth. Tillery, not satisfied with disgracing the sport of boxing a couple of moments earlier, was still taunting Bowe from a distance. Bowe, still very in the moment, attempted to get over to Tillery's location. By this time there was a good forty-five people in the ring and that simply was not going to happen. The crowd was in a frenzy over what they had just witnessed. The crowd seemed in shock about the turn of events but also seemed disgruntled about the fight not continuing. Tillery, on a streak of odd and uncanny behavior, jumped up onto the turnbuckle, pumped his arms in the air, and was met with a chorus of boos. From start to finish, the last fifteen minutes had been one of the craziest scenes in the history of the sport. Some in attendance were disputing why Elijah would be disqualified. That particular argument is with out base. Committing a foul as heinous as kicking someone after the bell is surefire grounds for being disqualified. Tillery, in the opinion of some, was looking for a way out of the fight. He found it by instigating a shameless sequence of events.

**Thell Torrence:** **I was actually in the back with Wayne McCullough, getting him ready, when the fight began. Once I had done that, I peeked out from the dressing room to watch a little bit of the first round. For some reason I had to go back into the dressing room, but from there I could hear a lot of noise and confusion. I got out to take a look, and there is this entire ruckus going on, it was crazy, but I actually was not in the**

ring when everything went down. From a distance, it was something to see. The crowd could not believe what had happened. I remember Bowe coming back to the dressing room angry. We were lucky that the incident did not get out hand.

Mr. Jones: First of all, Rock Newman screwed me in that fight. He told me I would get to announce the main event, and he played me. It was pretty grimy. That fight was out of control. I remember everyone in the crowd going apeshit because they didn't agree that the fight should been stopped. People paid good money to see the fight, and before they knew it, the fight was over. I also don't understand why Rock Newman would jump onto the ring mat. That's when everything got crazy. For a second I thought there might be a riot. Tillery fell on a lot of people when he went over the ropes. He actually injured Ms. Commissioner in the process. She retired on the amount of money she was awarded due to that incident.

This unfortunate incident would not be the last time Riddick would be involved in an event of pure pandemonium. Many have used this incident as an indictment on Bowe's camp. Some are critical of the seemingly volatile nature of the people Bowe had surrounded himself with. It is almost humorous in retrospect. Bowe's camp reacted to the developing situation opposed to causing it. Rock Newman, who many believed escalated the incident, was guilty of no such thing. Riddick Bowe was a couple of wins away from a title eliminator; the stakes had never been higher for Rock Newman's fighter. Rock had every right to protect his investment along with sticking up for his friend. From an athlete's point of view, Rock's actions were the ultimate display of loyalty. Tillery could have very easily injured Riddick's knee with those street fighter roundhouse kicks. Elijah could have delayed his ascent up the heavyweight ranks. All things considered, Rock's reaction to the situation makes perfect sense, if you are Rock Newman. The fight, while being a black eye on the sport, generated national interest. The shine had nothing to do with the actual fight.

It had everything to do with the circus that followed the fight. It made perfect boxing sense to stage a rematch.

The rematch was set for December 13, 1991, two months after the fiasco in Washington DC. The national attention of the first encounter gave the second fight relative notoriety; most thought the additional hype was supplemented by the volatile nature of both camps. How the fighters matched up in the ring was almost incidental. Given the events of the last fight, one would think that Bowe would come out like gangbusters in the first round. It was not so. Bowe began the first round somewhat lethargic. He seemed a step slow in his initial attempt to walk down Elijah. Elijah started the fight actually fighting a tough, disciplined, tight fight. He was outjabbing Riddick, he was out timing Riddick, and he was using impressive movements to keep Riddick off balance for the entire first round. Elijah clearly won the first round. He put some mustard on the situation when the round concluded. Tillery raised his hands in victory after the bell rang; it almost seemed that he was trying to convince himself that the first round was a precursor to the entire fight. The second round was not much more eventful than the first. Bowe did a better job of cutting off the ring and landed some decent body shots. Tillery meanwhile had regressed from effective movement to effective bicycle riding. While he had seemed sharp in the first round, the body attack being mounted by Bowe was already bearing some fruit. In the fourth round, it became evident to Elijah, and the crowd, that Big Daddy had finally warmed up. Thirty seconds into the round, Bowe landed a classic overhand right, catching Elijah in the midst of throwing a right hand of his own. The punch rocked Tillery's head back and elicited a big gasp from the crowd. Bowe seized the moment, attacking Elijah with countless power shots. Elijah tried to fend off the offensive by keeping both gloves directly in front of his face. Bowe, in an impressive tactical display, went to the body first, ripping shots on Tillery's sides, waiting for those gloves to drop. When they did, he ripped an uppercut that made Elijah turn his head completely around and rest his head on the ropes, covered by his gloves. It was the ultimate sign of submission. The referee, for reasons that elude even the most schooled boxing mind, did not call the fight at that stage. He gave Elijah a standing eight count. A standing eight count is well within the rules in the state of New Jersey, but to onlookers, Elijah's body language after the uppercut told everyone that he had all the punishment he needed. It was time to call the fight. Elijah, with blood pouring out is his nose, took the eight count and was asked by the referee if he wanted to continue. Elijah made the right decision and admitted he could not. Elijah was helped to his corner by the referee. It had been a brutal and emphatic statement by Bowe. It had been an easy work for Riddick; it had amounted to a light sparring session.

The second fight went the way the first fight would have ended. Elijah Tillery was only given relevance and a subsequent rematch because he has made a spectacle of himself in the first fight. Some have said the punishment Bowe laid on Elijah marked the beginning of the end for Tillery's tenure as a professional boxer. Tillery would fight only one more time two years later; he suffered a sixth-round knockout at the hands of James Smith. Tillery encountered legal problems after retirement, which should come as no surprise given his odd behavior between the ropes. Tillery was a speed bump that turned into a stop sign for Riddick. There is no way in the world that Bowe and his handlers thought they would see Tillery twice when they initially signed to fight him. The rematch made boxing sense, that is for sure, but there was truly no upside to it outside of capitalizing on the national attention of the first fiasco, and of course padding Bowe's record as he prepared for the last leg of his title run

# 9

# Juicy

The year 1992 would be the biggest year of Riddick Bowe's life. It would be the year that would etch him in the annals of boxing history. Bowe had emerged on the heavyweight scene. He was ready to stake his claim to the heavyweight title. It had been a long journey for the Brownsville native; he had endured poverty, the passing of family members, failing to win a gold medal at the Olympics, and of course all the negativity in the air about how he conducted himself. Bowe's emergence on the scene came at a time when the heavyweight title was a point of much debate. There was an undisputed heavyweight champion; his name was Evander Holyfield. Evander had taken the title from Buster Douglas two years earlier; Evander was two fights into his reign as heavyweight champion. James "Buster" Douglas had defied 42–1 odds, ripping the titles from Mike Tyson in the most shocking upset in boxing history. The shock wave that Buster victory created manifested a ripple effect that would reach Riddick Bowe and his destiny to become world champion. This was an unexpected turn of events for the heavyweight division; it was thought that Mike Tyson would hold the titles until a summit meeting with Evander Holyfield could be arranged. Mike Tyson, who many saw as the real heavyweight champion, had run into an opponent he could not beat: the law.

In July of 1991, Tyson was arrested in connection with the rape of an eighteen-year-old beauty queen at a pageant in Indianapolis, Indiana. Mike went on to be tried and convicted of the crime. Mike Tyson was sentenced to prison for six years. Indirectly, this chain of events laid the groundwork for Riddick to challenge Evander the following year. The world had been waiting for Tyson-Holyfield to take place for years. The two were scheduled to tangle in the fall of 1991, but Tyson pulled out of the fight due to a rib injury. The fight did not get a chance to be put back together due to Tyson's rape conviction and subsequent jail sentence.

Even though the Holyfield fight was not the next fight, the fluid nature of the heavyweight division had cleared a path to the top for Bowe.

He began the year with early knockouts of average heavyweights Conroy Nelson and Everett "Big Foot" Martin. Bowe then signed to fight a vaunted title eliminator. Modern prizefighting is different than it was during the days of the Jack Dempsey, as it relates to titles, and the process in which a contender goes about becoming a world champion. During the days of the Great Depression and Eleanor Roosevelt, the heavyweight title was one belt. One champion, one king of the hill. In the modern era of boxing, there are several title belts; along with those different belts come separate sanctioning bodies. These sanctioning bodies all have rules and regulations. The sanctioning entities individually govern their specific belt. They keep themselves in the financial loop by appointing mandatory challengers. These appointments garner them fees. They also charge the champion a fee every time he fights. The sanctioning bodies have complete power over their rankings. With the advent of superchampions and interim titles, the sanctioning bodies are much worse now than they were then. The sanctioning bodies, in the modern-era boxing, are the source of 95 percent of corruption that goes on within the sport. They are an evil that every fighter must deal with if they hope to become a world champion. A champion, for example, will be mandated to fight a certain fighter by a certain date or risk being stripped of that belt. It becomes complicated when you have a unified champion because at any given time, a unified champion can have two and three mandatories that they must face. A mandatory challenger usually has that distinction bestowed upon him by the sanctioning body due to his specific merit. He may have been the number one contender for a long period, or the sanctioning body will organize a fight between their two top contenders for the right to be appointed the mandatory for the champion's belt. The fight between Riddick Bowe and Pierre Coetzer on July 18, 1992 was an example of such a juncture. The sanctioning body in this instance was the World Boxing Association. Evander Holyfield held the WBA's version of the heavyweight title. Therefore he was inclined to fight the winner of the fight at some point in the near future. Pierre Coetzer was actually the International Boxing Federation's number one ranked contender. Somehow he was being duped into fighting for the WBA's number one position. Why Coetzers handlers agreed to surrender a pole position ranking to contest another is a mystery. It was a gigantic opportunity for Bowe and, potentially, could land him the biggest fight of his life. Since it could land him a massive opportunity, the Coetzer encounter was a massive fight.

The fight would be broadcast on boxing's flagship station, HBO. Home Box Office, besides producing *True Blood*, is the straw that stirs the boxing drink. To this day, the network is as powerful as any one promoter or sanctioning body. HBO, to the chagrin of some, controls the direction of the sport and deeply influences the American boxing consumer. To perform positively on the network would do wonders for Bowe from a PR standpoint. HBO's primetime broadcast would vault Bowe into the living rooms of the viewing American public. The fight had galactic-sized implications for Bowe financially and professionally. He had achieved relevance in becoming a top ten heavyweight and taking part in a heavyweight eliminator. It was clear he was a solid contender, but in the world of boxing, being a contender and becoming a superstar are two different worlds completely. Bowe and his camp realized that millions and millions of dollars were on the table, possibly a heavyweight title reign. Standing in the champ's way was a bulldozer of a fighter in Pierre Coetzer. Pierre is one of those fighters in the mold of the great Roberto Duran, a slugger with slight sophistication. Pierre Coetzer knew how to box, but he would rather fight. Pierre was not a journeyman heavyweight whose best days were behind him; he was a duly tested veteran who finally had a chance to burst onto the scene with an impressive victory.

# 10
# South Africa

Politics and race can inflame any boxing promotion. Some of the biggest fights in history have been intertwined with the issues of race and politics. Jerry Cooney-Larry Holmes, Ali-Frazier 1, and who could forget Joe Louis-Max Schmeling. Riddick Bowe's fight with Pierre Coetzer would not scrape the sky like fights of the past. But it did bring to light a political issue that many had taken notice of. When the fight was initially announced, a press conference was called to promote the fight. This is a clockwork aspect of any boxing promotion of relative relevance. During the presser, tempers flared between both camps. Usually during these pressers, the promoters for both fighters will make an opening statement in an attempt to sell the fight to the media and fans. It can only be compared to a sales pitch. During Rock Newman's pitch, Coetzer's camp took exception to a reference Rock made to the apartheid.

The apartheid was a nefarious system of government that was employed by the National Party of South Africa. The apartheid called for complete segregation of Afrikaans, blacks, and Indians. The vast majority of the South African population was black, but the ruling and prevailing race of people were white. Bathroom signs or newspaper editorials did not imply the apartheid; it was an official government policy brought into legislation following the election of 1948. Although many countries practiced segregation, and in some cases slavery (North America), South Africa seemingly trumped all comers due to the legislative and organized nature of their social convictions. The fact that these convictions lasted well into the twenty-first century made it worse. This hurt South Africa in the world's political arena. South Africa also took a hit in the world of sports. Athletes of every creed, race, size, and shape refused to travel to South Africa to compete. In some cases, athletes refused to profit professionally in any way if there was somehow a connection to South Africa. Don King, who to this day preaches black unity to secure fight contracts, was one of the few exceptions to this unorganized movement. Pierre Coetzer, meanwhile, was not someone who campaigned for the continuation of this ugly form of government; he was not a high-ranking official within the NP, in fact he suffered because of the apartheid. For years Pierre Coetzer fought in absolute obscurity due to the fact that his top tier contemporaries either refused to travel to South Africa or refused to fight him altogether. Boycotting South Africa was the thing to do, and no one knew that more than Pierre Coetzer. The accounts vary on what exactly what Rock said to jumpstart the drama. While Rock was in midpitch, a high-ranking member of Pierre's camp approached the podium, shouting at Rock to not inject politics into this particular sporting event. Rock remained subdued, until the man would not sit down. Rock Newman exploded, telling the man to sit down, telling him, "You can tell black men in your country what to do, but you're not going to tell me what to do, because in this country, at least we free black men." This incited a good amount of commotion at the press conference, and the two camps had to be separated. There was some irony lost in the drama. The two fighters, the two men who eventually would punch each other in the face, were quite tranquil and cordial to each other throughout the memorable proceedings. Never mind that one was black and the other was white. In the wake of the presser, many were critical of Rock Newman and his outburst. One has to believe that Rock was standing up for what he believed in. No matter what anyone says, the social and political structure of South Africa for the longest time was simply unacceptable.

An old boxing adage is that styles make fights. Every fight unto itself is a self-contained drama based on the stylistic disposition of the two combatants. Every so often you get two fighters whose styles are a perfect match. This fight was one of those fights. Riddick Bowe, at this point in the boxing scene, may have been the biggest puncher in the sport pound for pound. Pierre Coetzer, on the other hand, was boxing's version of the immovable object. He came forward, took your punches, and the came forward again. Pierre Coetzer was going to get to you and hurt you, and he was willing to walk through Death Valley to do it. On paper, the fight was a delightful prospect for any true boxing fan. Riddick Bowe tangled with Pierre Coetzer on July 18, 1992. He would make a career high purse of $180,000. Both fighters were expected to bring offensive fireworks to the table. The expectation was proven correct. The opening round was truly a breathtaking stanza. Pierre Coetzer showed zero trepidation about walking right into the pocket with a superior puncher.

Bowe was happy to accommodate Pierre, and free-flowing firepower was the result. Bowe landed some earth-shattering shots in the opening round that would have made a lesser man quit. The punishment appeared to give Coetzer confidence. Pierre landed some notable punches of his own, gaining some respect. Pierre had put Riddick Bowe on notice; all roads to Evander Holyfield would require true commitment. The two went back and forth, each giving as good as they got, and confirming their matchup was worthy of the HBO stage. As the bell sounded, the crowd in attendance rose to their feet, applauding the two fighters for such a fierce display of the pugilistic science.

That would be the theme of the fight. Pierre coming forward and Riddick punishing him for doing so. Pierre Coetzer's valor, however, would become a taxable flaw as Riddick opened a pair of nasty cuts above Pierre's eyes. To be wounded in such a battle was bad news for Coetzer. Pierre, despite his visual disadvantages, continued to press forward, throwing caution to the wind, taking some vicious shots in the process. It began to get to the point where a stoppage in the fight seemed like the ethical thing to in the interest of Pierre's long-term health. Pierre, with all of his problems, simply would not give in or give up. The South Afrikaner was limited in terms of his talent but gifted as it pertained to his resolve. All the resolve in the world, however, could not compensate for repeated flush power shots to the head. Pierre's eyes were closing, and Bowe was beginning to take advantage, really hurting Coetzer in every exchange. The swelling around Pierre's eyes progressed to the point where he could not see any punches coming. Riddick Bowe's talent was becoming evident to those in attendance and those viewing at home on HBO. Something else became evident to those viewing the fight in person and at home. At some point during the bout, Riddick Bowe's trunks had developed a rip in the back of them. The rip would become so pronounced that Riddick's buttocks would be in plain view for most of the fight. It was an amusing anecdote for a truly violent event.

As his mind began to give in, Pierre was moving a little slower; he managed even less head movement than he did at the onset. The end of the fight and what precipitated it would become the subject of much debate afterward. In the sixth round, Bowe was deducted a point by referee Mills Lane for a brutal low blow that sent Pierre down to his knees and caused a five-minute delay. Pierre attempted to compose himself. The low blow was compounded by the fact that Bowe also landed a hook to the side of the head, even though it appeared that Coetzer was already down. Bowe claimed the low blow an accident when asked about it later. Coetzer's camp saw it as a dirty foul that disrupted any chance of Pierre winning the fight. The seventh and final round was inhumane at times; sometimes it was the left hook, sometimes it was the right hook, and there were also uppercuts that lifted Pierre's feet off the canvas. Pierre was being beaten up; he was unable to get out of the way or mount a credible offensive. The last fifteen seconds of the round were open for discussion. Bowe landed a hard right hand to the body followed by a strafing uppercut. Pierre's reaction to the punch was to disengage and turn around, cowering on his side. It appeared to everyone that he was appealing for a low-blow ruling. It appeared to Bowe that he was hurt. Riddick landed an overhead right that hurt Pierre badly, causing him to stumble against the ropes. Bowe followed with a mean right hand to the body and another right hand upstairs. Pierre was done. Mills Lane stepped in and called a halt to the action at 2:59 of the seventh round. Pierre Coetzer and his camp disputed the conclusion of the fight, arguing that the end of the bout was set in motion by another low blow. That was open to debate. Mills Lane, who is one of the most respected referees in the history of the sport, made the ruling, and according to the rules, the referee's decision prevails no matter what the circumstances. A disenchanted camp can file an official protest with the concerned commission; that process, however, is time consuming and not a sure thing. Pierre and his camp knew they would have to eat the decision and chose not to protest. The ruling, however, to many did not matter. Bowe was putting a world-class ass whupping on Pierre, and the result of the fight was academic. Taking into account the cuts, the swelling, and the clean power punching, it was hard to imagine Pierre making it to tenth round let alone the conclusion of the twelfth. Between every round in the second half of the fight, there had been two commissioned doctors supervising the proceedings in Pierre's corner. It is fair to surmise that Bowe may have hit Pierre low a second time; however, it made no difference in the end of the fight. Pierre was going to be knocked out, either technically or actually.

# 11
# Title Shot

Bowe had done it. Riddick Lamont Bowe had won the right to challenge for the undisputed heavyweight championship of the world. There were many pundits initially that figured this possibility was remote at best. There was no way in the world that someone with Riddick Bowe's emotional constitution could ever climb the heavyweight mountain. He had conquered all comers. Now it was time to cash in. It was this fight with Evander Holyfield that would jettison him down the road toward boxing immortality. The other thing that Bowe had accomplished during this joyous night was an amazing debut on Home Box Office. HBO loves fighters that sport magnetic personalities and produce drama. Riddick had given the network all of these things the night he knocked out Coetzer. HBO had streamed Riddick Bowe into American homes, and Bowe had delivered (with Pierre's help) an all-action battle that culminated in a stoppage victory. Bowe had showcased his prolific offensive skill set. He also at times had given the world a glimpse of his affable personality. He even had been conversating with the HBO broadcast booth over the course of the bout. The final result was a personable contender with the skills, the momentum, and the timing to take the heavyweight championship of the world from Evander Holyfield.

**Ken Sanders:** Evander Holyfield was one of the greatest fighters of all time. He was the perfect blend of speed and skill. He also had power. But his biggest trait was his heart. He had a bigger heart than any athlete that ever lived. Ever. He did nothing to undermine his career. No drinking or smoking or any bad habits of any kind. Never in twenty-five years of knowing the man has he ever been a problem. Always on time to the gym, always gives 100 percent. Evander, at that point in his career, was about as good as it got in boxing. No question he was the number one

> pound-for-pound fighter in the world going into the fight with Riddick Bowe.

Evander Holyfield, like Riddick Bowe, had many critics. Some felt that Evander was a blown-up cruiserweight masquerading as heavyweight. Evander's boxing pedigree, however, could not be questioned. He was a two-division champion at a relatively young age. He had all the makings of a true boxing superstar. He was an Olympic silver medalist; he very easily could have been a gold medalist if it were not for the worst call in Olympic boxing history. Despite the howler at the 1984 Olympics, Holyfield ran through the cruiserweight division, winning a title in only his fourteenth pro fight. He promptly made the decision to move up to the heavyweight division. In the history of boxing, no man had held the cruiserweight championship and then gone on to win the undisputed heavyweight championship. Evander accomplished that feat with haste, winning the undisputed heavyweight title within two years of entering the division.

**Jeffery Shultz:** Evander started out pumping gas at a small private airport. He started making pretty good money right out of the 1984 Olympics because it was a pretty vaunted Olympic class. Evander also was voted the MVP of the US Olympic team by the other boxers even though he was one of the few to *not* win a gold medal. Most believed he was robbed because of an unjust disqualification by the referee for hitting after the break. That, and the fact that he was humble, not flashy, and kind of country, made him a popular figure. Holyfield will tell you one of the toughest fights he ever had was beating Dwight Muhammad Qawi for the cruiserweight title in 1986, that at one point, he just wanted to finish the fight. But winning that decision is what started to earn him a reputation as being a guy who fought on heart and desire. He became a heavyweight two years later.

Evander was world renowned for his grit and seemingly endless reservoir of intestinal fortitude. Evander was a heavyweight with a true Napoleon complex. He was determined to prove that size does not matter at all times. This led him sometimes to abandon his superb boxing skills and brawl for the sake of pride. Evander also was celebrated because of his ability to rapidly recover. Evander had the ability to be in trouble and then explode on an unsuspecting opponent. In his fight with Bert Cooper, Holyfield had been knocked down early in the second round. He was seemingly out on his feet until he caught Bert with a counter hook, almost stopping Bert Cooper in the same round. He went on to stop Bert Cooper a couple rounds later. Evander Holyfield had an addiction to action-packed fights. It's what made him compelling to watch and, subsequently, an HBO darling. Evander was the heavyweight champion of the world; he already was one of the most accomplished fighters of his generation. Evander would enter the fight at the apex of his career. It was going to take one hell of a man to defeat him, or perhaps someone a little bigger. Before the fight could completely materialize, however, boxing's evil wizard waved his magic wand. Don King and the World Boxing Council would attempt to upset the applecart like only they can.

Evander Holyfield held several versions of the heavyweight title representing the numerous sanctioning bodies. Among those titles was the WBC heavyweight title. Beneath the surface, some believe that any WBC championship belt in any weight class is fair game for Don King. With Mike Tyson in jail and Evander Holyfield reigning, Don King was desperate for a heavyweight champion. He had enjoyed a silent monopoly over the heavyweight division going on almost twenty years. Naturally, King wanted his enterprise to continue. Buster Douglas had disrupted all of that, and here was Evander Holyfield continuing the trend. Don's only recourse was to put the pressure on Evander politically, much like he had Buster in Japan. King's avenging angel for such ventures is World Boxing Council president "for life" Jose Saluiman. Jose Sulaiman is reviled by some in the boxing world. He is not an evil person by any stretch but has furnished an infinite amount of questionable decisions during his self-appointed dictatorship. He has presided over the WBC for five decades. Going back to the seventies, Don King and Jose Sulaiman have given credibility to the notion that boxing is a corrupt industry. Many have dismissed the motion picture *The Great White Hype* as a slight exaggeration. The cartoon nature of the feature is not a far cry from what is rumored to take place between the two men. Many observers have hypothesized that some type of special relationship exists. Mind you, this special relationship is not as special as Bill Clinton and Tony Blair's. Time and time again through the years, the WBC has made incongruous decisions that seem to give Don King's stable of fighters a leg up over the concerned competition. Even when the WBC heavyweight champion is not a Don King fighter, they are still indirectly dictated too by Mr. King. The favoritism shown towards Don King's fighters by the WBC is shameless and consistent. Most of the shady machinations over the years are specific to the heavyweight division. Many heavyweights have suffered or benefited from the Menchai that goes on between Don King Productions and the WBC. In 1978, Leon Spinks had not been the WBC champion for fifteen minutes before he felt the invisible hand of Don King. Citing outlandish reasons, the president "for life" forced him to vacate his title. That title was subsequently contested between Ken Norton and Larry Holmes, two Don King fighters. This shrewd move assured Don King that he would control a piece of the heavyweight title even though Ali, who was a Don King fighter, had been defeated by Leon Spinks just a couple weeks before. The WBC for no reason at all took Spinks's title and made sure the WBC heavyweight champion would be a Don King fighter. When Mike Tyson did finally get out of jail in 1995, he was installed as the number one contender in the WBC ranking, despite three years of inactivity. Mike Tyson's first foe out of jail, Peter Mckneely, a club fighter, was placed in the top ten of the WBC rankings before the fight. It was true to a famous scene from *The Great White Hype*.

With no claim to the heavyweight title, and Mike Tyson a guest of the government, Don King began to line things up for his eventual release. When Main Events made it public that Evander Holyfield was going to fight Riddick Bowe, the WBC notified Evander that he could be stripped if he chose to fight Bowe instead of Razor Ruddock. Razor Ruddock was a Don King fighter, as luck would have it. Evander Holyfield and Shelly Finkel countered with a court order that forced the WBC to cease and desist. This occurrence, and many other happenings, would lead to a federal investigation. Senate subcommittees and national attention followed. Evander Holyfield, on tape, told investigators that the WBC wanted him to fight Razor Ruddock because he was a Don King fighter. Luckily for Riddick Bowe, the comings and goings of Don King and Jose Sulaiman did not prevent his dream from becoming a reality.

Evander Holyfield's court order stood up, and Riddick Bowe's title shot would go on as planned.

To make a fight between two high-profile American fighters is always a fable unto itself. Riddick Bowe was the number one contender on the precipice of boxing nirvana. The feeling in boxing inner circles was that Holyfield had not yet fought a young fresh heavyweight with size. Riddick Bowe, in challenging for the title, would provide skeptics with the litmus test they had been waiting for. The two men were not strangers to one another. They had sparred in their younger years when Evander was cleaning up the 190-pound division. These clandestine battles had given both combatants a good account of the other. There is no scouting report like sparring.

**Riddick Bowe:** **Evander is tough. I knew that from our sparring sessions. I knew he would not back down from my power, and I knew I had better defend myself. He gave me the business during those sparring sessions, but that was then, this was now, and at this point in my mind, I was the better fighter. He was a professional during our sparring sessions. I was still an amateur. I knew this time would be different. I was a professional now. A hungry professional.**

The two sides quickly began negotiations and reached a complicated agreement. This promotion would be the first of many times that Rock Newman and the late but great Dan Duva of Main Events would do business together. It would not always be a smooth ride. The rigorous attention to detail that Rock Newman brought to the table could be difficult to deal with.

**Kathy Duva:** **I have a general recollection that Rock and Dan were constantly at odds and that Rock was quite particular about how Bowe was portrayed in the media and every aspect of the promotion. This led to many shouting matches between my late husband and Rock. I recall that HBO had to photo-**

> shop Bowe's photo to slim him down for one of the Holyfield-Bowe posters because he was pretty out of shape when we held the press conference to announce the fight, and Rock was unhappy about the way he looked in his photo. If it wasn't one thing, it was the other. It was never ending

The contract stated that Bowe would indeed get a shot at the heavyweight title. But the title shot would come with stipulations. The first stipulation mandated that Main Events Inc. would copromote three of Bowe's future fights. They would also get a 28 percent cut of all promotional fees. Bowe didn't sell his soul, but he perhaps left more on the table than he needed too. Three fights is roughly a year and a half for a top-level prizefighter, unless your name is Vitali Klitschko. To get into bed with a major promoter is understandable when you are the B side of the promotion. While seeming obscure, this little footnote would cause a little drama for Bowe later on in his career. Riddick Bowe would make a career high $3,000,000 to challenge Evander, plus an upside of the PPV buys per the amount of subscriptions that the telecast generated. HBO would spotlight the bout as a TVKO main event. Before HBO PPV would become a staple of the industry, TVKO was the primary PPV carrier for the network. The stage would be as bright as boxing had seen since Mike Tyson was king. The fun and games of being a rising prospect were at an end. The days of being the next big thing were over. Riddick Bowe's time seemingly had come. He would only realize this moment if he was in shape. Rock Newman had made some reforms to the infrastructure of Riddick Bowe's camp before the Pierre Coetzer fight. One of these reformations would come in the form tiny little magician named Mackie Shilstone.

Mackie Shilstone is quite possibly the most respected personal trainer in the United States of America. Then and right now. His influence stretches to the furthest parts of the sport universe. The client that put Mackie on the map was Hall of Famer Michael Spinks. Shilstone was instrumental in Spinks's heavyweight rise. He played a huge role in Spinks's lifting the heavyweight title from Hall of Famer Larry Holmes in June 1983. What made Mackie's role so glamorous was the fact that Spinks had campaigned as a light heavyweight and moved up two full divisions to heavyweight. Mackie's regimen beefed up Spinks and took him to unprecedented heights. Rock Newman had been Michael Spinks's publicist during those formative years and was familiar with Mackie personally. As Riddick Bowe began to climb the heavyweight ranks, the persistent questions about his training camps were enough to provoke Newman to act. Mackie joined the team and made impact right away. Mackie's goal with Bowe was simple and straightforward. Reshape his bad habits and push him to the next level of physical excellence.

**Mackie Shilstone:** Me getting involved with Riddick Bowe actually went way back to 1982 when I worked with the then light heavyweight champion Michael Spinks. It just so happened that Rock Newman was the publicist for that camp. Rock Newman saw what I did. He watched me take the light heavyweight champion to the heavyweight division. Rock saw me help Michael Spinks defeat undisputed heavyweight champion Larry Holmes. Rock Newman saw the ins and the outs of my work, and as Spinks started to head towards the end of his career, Riddick Bowe was starting to rise. Rock Newman made a decision that he wanted to get involved in promotion. He took a chance and went all in with Riddick Bowe. He brought Riddick to me, not in the hospital that I currently work at, but a different hospital. This was back in 1989. I helped Riddick get himself together after the Olympics. He had some orthopedic issues and some weight issues, so I was the person to help him through all that when he returned from Korea and subsequently signed with Rock. At one point, Riddick even lived in the hospital I worked out of. Rock realized that working with me extensively at such an early stage of Bowe's career was not cost-effective. We actually did not work together for a while as Rock was attempting to build Riddick's career. Rock made all the right choices in the infant stages of Bowe's career. He made the right fights, and he made them at the right time. The next time that I was brought in to work with Bowe was the Pierre Coetzer fight. The winner of this fight would be the number one contender for the heavyweight championship, which was owned by Evander Holyfield. Rock came to me and said, "Look, I cannot afford a lot but could use your help." I agreed to join camp and we beat Pierre Coetzer. Rock brought me back for the title fight. We trained for that fight in Bend, Oregon. In that camp, I trimmed thirty pounds off Bowe. Riddick went into the fight weighing 235 pounds, and he was in phenomenal shape. We knew that Evander thought he could tire Bowe out after about eight rounds, but with Bowe coming in at such a good weight, Evander was not able to use that strategy to win the fight. I worked with Spinks when he fought Jerry Cooney, and we knew that we could tire Jerry out after a certain amount of time. I was sure that Evander was going to employ the same plan of attack when taking on Riddick Bowe. In knowing this, I used all types of innovative techniques. The Riddick Bowe that Evander would see that night was unlike anything Holyfield had ever seen.

Any successful training camp is not just limited to nutrition and conditioning applications. The boxing side of things needs to be in tune as well. Bowe's camp in Oregon in the fall of 1992 satisfied this requirement.

Thell Torrence: The program to get ready for that fight was well organized and well carried out. The sparring partners that Rock brought in good were strong guys. The tone of camp was among the best we have ever had. Riddick was ready to get the job done, we actually brought in smaller fighters. One was a cruiserweight to get Riddick ready for the task of tracking Evander's rhythm and movement. Things went great in training camp. Riddick was so in tune, and working so hard, that there was no doubt in our minds that he was going to win the fight. Evander put up the fight we were expecting, but he was not really prepared to deal with a big man that had the fundamentals of Riddick. Riddick also had been sparring with quick smaller guys, so it was not as if he had trouble finding Evander. Bowe was already becoming a great fighter, but in that fight, on that stage, he transitioned from a boy to a man. He became a man in that fight.

The night of November 13, 1992 stands on its own in the pantheon of boxing lore. Many fights over the course of heavyweight history have produced images that endure. Jess Willard stopping Jack Johnson. Joe Louis defeating Max Schmelling for race and country. Every now and again there is a fight that captures just how beautiful the sweet science can be. This was to be such an occasion.

The stakes had never been higher for Bowe. Riddick went about his business accordingly. Everything was on the line. Bowe could go from a highly touted prospect to worldwide superstar in the blink of an eye. The transformation would not come without tax. Evander Holyfield, on top of his pedigree and talent, was carrying a major league chip on his shoulder. Evander had been champion for over two years, but to the public, his reign left something to be desired. In Evander's initial campaign as heavyweight champion, his schedule led some to believe he was being protected. The general belief was that every name on his heavyweight docket was tragically flawed in some way. Buster Douglas was fat, Bert Cooper was short, and George Foreman was old. Before he defended his titles against Riddick, Holyfield struggled with a forty-year-old Larry Holmes en route to an unimpressive twelve-round decision. His title defense against Larry Holmes was lackluster and gave his critics ammunition. Evander would not be truly accepted as a legitimate heavyweight champion until he defeated a big strong prime heavyweight. Yes, there were questions about Bowe's mental toughness because he had never been into the top-level cauldron. But we must all admit that the burden of proof was on Evander as well; could he finally defeat a real heavyweight? Both men had something to prove. Given this projected climate, it was hard to understand how many at the time did not foresee the war that was about to take place.

    Several years before they would meet for the heavyweight title, Riddick Bowe had been a sparring partner in Evander's training camps. At the time, Bowe was a gangly up-and-comer while Evander was campaigning in the cruiserweight division. These sessions were easy work for Evander. Holyfield was clearly the more polished product at that point. Evander told some of those around him that Bowe had serviceable tools but lacked the endurance to ever really be a danger down the road. Evander did not really respect the possibility that this lazy giant would really have the heart to take the title. It was a highly arrogant disposition in retrospect. Evander should have studied the film. The genesis of Evander's attitude came in those years they sparred together. This lack of apprehension laid the foundation for an upset. Evander Holyfield saw Riddick Bowe no different than he saw George Foreman or Bert Cooper.

**Evander Holyfield:** Lou Duva had allowed Bowe to get some work in at my camp when he was still an up-and-comer. He was a good guy. I liked him a lot. There were a couple sparring sessions in which he gave me a little business, but he would always run out of gas. When the fight was made, I knew it was going to be tough, but I figured he would not have the stamina to compete with me for twelve rounds. Maybe that was a mistake, but I had seen Bowe in sparring, and he was not always in world championship shape.

Kathy Duva: When Evander won the title, I remember my husband telling me that there were only three guys in the entire division that could beat Evander: Lennox Lewis, Michael Moore, and Riddick Bowe. Dan would tell me that Bowe's physical dimensions along with his punching power would be a huge problem for Evander should they ever meet. This was well in advance of the first fight and proved to be logical reasoning. Dan knew we would eventually have to fight all of them but was not necessarily in a rush to do so. Dan was a good matchmaker and put off the fight with Bowe as long as he could.

# 12

# And New . . .

**R**iddick Bowe's dressing room was filled with tension the night of November 13, 1992. Flanked by family members and his handlers, Bowe sat on the very cusp of superstar status. The young man from Brownsville, Brooklyn, hoped to eradicate the naysayers and bad wishers. Drenched in prayer, the entourage was brewing with differing agendas. Some members of the entourage were hoping for their coin cow to morph into a cash cow. They did not really care about Bowe accomplishing his dream, instead they were much more concerned about what victory could mean to their respective bottom lines. Rock Newman, a self-made man in the sport, sought to cement his status as a boxing titan. Rock had been in the game for about twelve years and had been waiting for this moment. Rock did a viable job of developing Bowe. He had been even more masterful moving Bowe along quickly. If Riddick Bowe defeated Evander Holyfield, it would be the second fastest ascension to the title in boxing history. Riddick Bowe, for all intents and purposes, had become a corporation. Rock had made the initial investment in the corporation. That made him, by definition, Bowe's senior partner. Rock had shown some true business acumen and considerable foresight to reach this point. His investment could do more than pay off, it could set him up for the rest of his life. At the time of the Holyfield fight, Rock Newman had invested roughly $300,000 into his fighter. Virtually the sum of his wealth. He had sold his car, borrowed from friends, and staked his life in the belief that Riddick Bowe would one day be heavyweight champion. He had taken a fighter that nobody wanted and brought him to the brink of superstardom. He had not sold out and given options to the major promoters along the way. He had seen the journey through and was now on destiny's doorstep. Riddick Bowe challenged for the heavyweight championship of the world that night, but what many don't understand was that so did Rock Newman. He was in the ring with Riddick Bowe emotionally. Everything had been building to this moment for Rock Newman and Riddick Bowe respectively.

A rags to riches is classic American theatre. With the help of TVKO, Riddick Bowe's version would be played out on the world's stage. An HBO official came into the dressing room and informed Bowe's camp that the undercard had concluded. It was time to prepare for his ring walk. Playing the role of the underdog should be a pressure-free situation; however, given his low-income roots and the fact that so many people doubted him for so long, there was pressure on Bowe. The moment had come; it was time to challenge for the undisputed heavyweight championship of the world.

**Riddick Bowe:** **All I could think about as I made my ring walk was all the hard work that had brought me to this point. All the training camps and the traveling and the short money purses had brought me to this fight. There was no doubt in my mind that I was going to win the fight. I knew in my heart that I was going to be crowned king of the boxing world on that night. When Buffer was introducing me, I remember thinking that I had made it. When he said his "Let's get ready to rumble," and the crowd roared, I got goose bumps. There is no feeling like that. I was so confident that it was my night. I remember Evander's eyes meeting with mine, and I could see in his eyes that he knew it was not going to be an easy night.**

The first round was tentative. That was to be expected given the magnitude of the event. Tense head movement and jabs dominated the first half of the first round. Bowe let Holyfield know very early on that he would have to contend with his jab in order to compete. Neither man seemed like he wanted to jump into an all-out war early. The punch output was measured. Evander, on his toes and moving, landed some meaningful right hands. Holyfield seemed to be getting the better of the action as the round evolved into its second half. Evander made an adjustment and began throwing combinations from a distance. The combinations gave Bowe trouble because he was having trouble finding Evander once Holyfield was done throwing. The fight began to open up in the last minute of the round as Bowe began to return fire and found some success doing so. Evander, the cagey champion, seemed determined not to back down or give Bowe a chance to land at the same time. The first round came to a close. Riddick Bowe appeared to be perplexed by the animal he had in front of him. It was clear that Evander was a different cut of cat than any opponent Riddick had faced thus far

**Riddick Bowe:** I was nervous in the first round. Maybe it was the size of the moment. I can't be sure. But that first round was all-nerves dog. I was a deer in the headlights at first; it had hit me just how big this fight was.

Evander did not rest on his laurels at the second round began. He was pressing the action and landing punches on the bigger man. Riddick, at this point in his career, had never seen someone with this type of skill. Riddick Bowe was content to try and time Holyfield until he made a mistake. The turning point of the fight, however, came as the result foul that was not called.

**Evander Holyfield:** Up until midway through the second round, I was fighting a tough disciplined fight. I had no intention of getting into a brawl of any kind. We knew that was Bowe's only chance to win, and I was not going to give him that chance. During one of our exchanges, Riddick hit me low, like really low, and he hit me with power. I looked at the referee wondering why he didn't call the foul. At that moment, Bowe began hitting me in the back of the head. That got under my skin. That's when I stopped boxing and started fighting.

**Joe Cortez:** I didn't think it was a low blow. It was close, but I didn't rule it low. Evander looked at me wondering why I didn't call anything. He clinched Bowe while he was looking at me, and at that moment I attempted to break them up. When I stepped towards them, they fought out of the clinch, and I backed up. The

> fight changed at that point. It was toe-to-toe action from that point on.

Riddick Bowe, on top of his size advantages, had a detailed mental scouting report of Evander's style. It is one thing to watch a tape, but when you sparred with your opponent prior to the fight, it gives a fighter a better sense of his foe's timing and habits.

**Riddick Bowe:** I knew from sparring that Evander liked to use his jab to get inside. Evander was tough and smart, so you had to be careful and not get lazy. I also remember from sparring that Evander liked to throw lead right hands. Every time he did that, I tried to counter him with the left hook. In the second round, he stopped boxing and started fighting. That's when the things started to go my way.

Evander Holyfield's frustration caused him to commit a tragic error. Evander was determined not to be bullied and fouled by the bigger man. Evander's emotions got the best of him. He decided to transition to fighting a phone booth fight. The term *phone booth* in boxing simply means there is no distance between the two fighters; they could fight in a phone booth if given the opportunity. Evander was catching punches and landing his own, but he was not catching every punch and, being outweighed by twenty pounds, was assuming quite a risk. The third round was a slugfest with the much larger Bowe getting the better of most of the exchanges. Bowe's punches began to take their effect, and Holyfield slowed down as Riddick began to speed up.

**Riddick Bowe:** That's when I knew there was no way he was going to be able to trade with me, and I know that he knew this as well. A realization like that is infuriating to a fighter with the heart of Evander. In his mind, he believed that he could outtough me, and after some of those right hands and left hooks, he realized that was not going to be the case tonight, baby.

Riddick Bowe would exacerbate Evander's anger by landing a second low blow (although he was not penalized for the first), and this time he was reprimanded by Joe Cortez in between rounds three and four. It's hard to determine if the blows were intentional, but they were turning the fight into something that Bowe could win, a gunfight. Bowe's guns were bigger and stronger than Holyfield's. Bowe was becoming a little too gung ho for Eddie Futch's liking, however. Eddie reminded Bowe to not walk into the pocket without throwing his jab. It was sound advice.

**Evander Holyfield:** As the fight wore on, the fight started to become tougher and tougher. I made the decision to fight him because I had lost my temper over the low blows. After a couple of rounds of banging, my eyes swelled up. I was also cut, which further impaired my vision. My corner was pleading with me to box, but I could not even see anything at that point. I had no choice but to stand in and fight this big rascal. Since I could not see him from a distance, fighting on the inside was the only way I had a chance to be effective.

**Larry Merchant:** There was a feeling on some people's part that Bowe was not really tough mentally, and subsequently, Holyfield defied the fight plan of George Benton. Evander made the decision that he was going to test Bowe's fortitude. He decided he was going to walk into the eye of the storm and see who was the toughest guy. That would prove to be a huge mistake because Bowe was a hungry younger fighter at that point. Riddick was able to stay with Holyfield and prove that he had the kind of toughness we admire in a heavyweight champion. Holyfield's decision to test his mettle backfired.

As the fight headed into the second half, Evander's reign atop the heavyweight division was under considerable pressure. He was hurt, he was having trouble seeing punches coming, and he was too darn stubborn to take one step back. He refused to acquiesce to Riddick's prevailing physical strength. As Bowe rose off his stool for the seventh round, the capacity crowd at the Thomas and Mack Center began to chant for

Bowe. Rock Newman allegedly started the cheer, but it was the first time in Bowe's career that his name had been chanted. Here it was, happening in his biggest fight to date.

**Riddick Bowe:** I had never heard that before. To have an entire arena shouting your name as one was a nice moment. It motivated me even more to snatch up them belts.

Bowe would hurt Holyfield for the first time in the fight in the 7th round. An overhand right that cleared Holyfield's shoulder, the punch landed flush and froze the heavyweight champion. Bowe didn't realize the depth of the damage at first, but quickly jumped on Evander, finally landing his vaunted uppercut. Evander in the midst of being assaulted, appeared to headbutt Bowe ever so slightly. Riddick Bowe, unfazed by the butt, marched right in and landed another flush right hand. Bowe was letting Holyfield know he was not out of the woods yet. Evander developed another cut in the 8th round. Riddick Bowe controlled the action in the round while loading up on right hands. He was catching Evander with power punches, but not cleanly enough to stop Evander. Over the next round and half, Evander found openings to score with counter right hands, but never to the point where he could blunt the Riddick Bowe express. Evander because of his ego, was inherently dangerous at all times. For the first time in Holyfield's title reign however, he appeared to be fading in a fight. It was the first time he had been truly tested in the heavyweight division by a bigger man. Bert Cooper had tested him, but lacked the size and skill to capitalize. Riddick Bowe was gaining momentum as the fight entered the 10th round.

Bowe stepped out for the tenth round and promptly landed stiff jab that moved Evander back about 2 ½ feet. Evander was clearly tiring and Bowe seemed to sense that he was ripe to be taken. Former heavyweight king George Foreman, on the call for HBO, told viewers that he believed Evander would fall sometime during the round. On the heels of George's imfamous words, lightining struck. As they were clinching, Riddick Bowe landed the uppercut of his life, completely stunning Holyfield and sending him on wobbly legs clear across Riddick. What would follow, would define both men. The tenth round to most fight fans, ranks amongst the greatest rounds in the history of the sport. Jim Lampley, on the call for HBO, called the sequence well

> **George Foreman thinks Holyfield is going down in this round, and Bowe stuns him with an uppercut, and JUST LIKE THAT, the champion… struggles to stay on his feet! Ducks one right hand, blocks another, Bowe throwing and throwing, Holyfield is hanging in there, what a heart by Holyfield. Joe Cortez watching, champion gets the benefit of the doubt."

Bowe threw a home run right hand that missed but managed to catch Evander with a grazing left that sent Holyfield into the corner almost going down. Riddick Bowe proceeded to punish Evander from all angles for the next minute of the round. How Evander Holyfield stayed on his feet through such a terrible pounding is amazing. Evander, throughout his reign, had shown the ability to come back from the dead; no matter what the level of adversity, he found a way to turn the tide. Riddick Bowe, despite his advantage, overplayed his hand.

**Riddick Bowe:** I caught him slipping in the clinch and landed that uppercut. I thought I had him. I was tapping that ass for a good minute. To his credit, he hung in there. To this day, I don't know how I didn't knock his ass out. I don't get it. My arms started to get tired from throwing so many punches, and I took a little break to get my wind back.

**Evander:** He hurt me real bad with that uppercut. I didn't know where I was for a little bit. I remember just trying to hang in and weather the storm. After awhile, I noticed that he was slowing down. At that moment, I knew I was going to be all right.

Forty seconds after being on the brink of disaster, Evander Holyfield had regained his senses and was returning fire. The toughness and valor that Evander displayed in the tenth round etched his name in boxing history. It silenced the naysayers that said he was a blown-up cruiserweight. The intensity of the round simmered for a minute while the two men attempted to regain their breath. Evander recuperated just a little faster than Riddick Bowe and took advantage of it. Evander jumped on Riddick Bowe, backing him with activity and landed punches. Jim Lampley continued to call the action flawlessly:

> "Look at Holyfield! What a warrior! Reversing the tide of the battle, and now he has Bowe wobbly, ANOTHER RIGHT HAND BY HOLYFIELD and another! Everyone in The Thomas and Mack center on their feet, Round ten continues after the bell."

It was the defining moment of Evander's career. Evander had Bowe in serious trouble in the final minute of the round to the point where Bowe almost tasted the canvas. The round was Rocky-like in the last ten seconds. During one of the defining exchanges in boxing history, they fought after the bell and lifted the roof off the Thomas and Mack Center.

Riddick Bowe: If you watch the tape, I give Evander a pat on the stomach at the end of the round. I was almost in awe of the heart this man had. I thought I had him; somehow he survived and hit me with some tough shots. What a round.

Joe Cortez: The tenth round is what stands out in my mind. Some have called it the round of the decade, even the century. Bowe had Holyfield almost out on his feet. He caught him with a shot and sent him into one of the turnbuckles. He caught him with that tremendous uppercut that he used to throw. Bowe went after Evander, almost stopping him. I came very close to calling the fight, one more clean shot, I would have called it. Some people have asked me over the years why I didn't stop it. In all my years of experience as a referee, I have learned that sometimes you have to do your homework and follow these fighters that you officiate. Because of Evander's experience, and the fact that he had shown an incredible ability to come back, he had earned the benefit of the doubt in my mind despite the fact the he appeared in big trouble. I made the right decision because Evander came back strong in that very round and went the distance. Evander got through the storm. I don't know how he did it, but once Bowe slowed down, Evander seemed to get his second wind. Bowe was clearly tired from throwing so many punches. Evander caught Bowe with some clean shots, and all of sudden, he had Bowe going. It was so amazing to so many people that Evander could come back from being in that kind of trouble and almost have Bowe out on his feet. To actually close out the round almost putting Bowe down, tremendous round.

Jim Lampley: Certainly the greatest round of heavyweight boxing I ever covered. I have a distinctive memory of being in my ringside position. Directly across the canvas was Earvin Magic Johnson. I lived in LA and covered the Lakers for nine years during their dynasty. We had been friends for a while, and he was a huge boxing fan. He was sitting there at ringside that night for the fight. When they went back to their corners after the tenth round, I caught Magic's eyes as he stood up with the rest of the crowd. He lifted his head back in the air and looked at me. It was almost like he could not believe what he just saw. No one could.

The eleventh round began as a fluid continuation of the tenth. The only difference, however, was that Evander appeared to be not fully recovered from his punch output in the previous round. Bowe took advantage, slamming Evander with a left hook that put the champ on Queer Street and sent him toward the ropes. Evander, even though he was hurt, managed to push Bowe back with his body into the ropes. Riddick Bowe slipped Evander's whole body seemingly and landed a jarring overhand right that appeared to strike Evander in the back of the head. A shot to the back of the head in boxing is known as a rabbit punch. It is illegal and sometimes can result in an immediate disqualification.

**Evander Holyfield:** He hit me in the back of the head. That's why I went down. I was hurt, but not to the point

> where I was going to go down. I didn't understand why the referee didn't take any points. That was the fourth or fifth foul he didn't call throughout the fight. It had me frustrated to be honest.

Joe Cortez has taken criticism from boxing fans and scribes throughout his career as a high-profile referee. His resume is not as incongruous as Richard Steele's, but many have taken objections to specific, independent judgments that he renders. The Ricky Hattons and Marcos Madinas of the world take objection to his unneeded involvement in the action. Evander on the other hand did not understand why he was not more involved. Evander was up against it. He was busted up, hurt, and seemingly not going to receive any favors from the referee. Riddick Bowe was stalking and landing. Riddick Bowe was finally breaking the famous will of Evander Holyfield. Evander was stumbling about the ring, looking like a beaten man. Jim Lampley remarked on the call that Evander appeared to be spent. He was. The conclusion of the fight was all but assured. Riddick Bowe was decisively beating Evander Holyfield. The only question that remained was if Evander would finish the fight on his feet or on his back.

The crowd rose to its feet at the beginning of the twelfth round to applaud the tremendous battle they were in the midst of. As the two fighters touched gloves, the crowd shouted its appreciation. The two combatants had shown legendary effort and courage. Riddick Bowe pushed a weakened Evander Holyfield around the ring. Evander was unable to respond and seemed resigned to the fact that the fight was out of reach. With the crowd chanting his name, Riddick Bowe punctuated his claim to the heavyweight championship by not allowing Evander to rest at any point during the final round. The crowd stood back up as the seconds ticked away on Evander Holyfield initial title reign. Then again this was Las Vegas; counting your boxing chickens in Sin City can be a futile endeavor. Riddick Bowe, the disrespected prospect from Brownsville, Brooklyn, has turned in the performance of his life.

Riddick Bowe did a victory lap around the ring. Rock Newman and Thell Torrence embraced Bowe. He breathed a sigh of relief. It had been a brutal war, and it appeared that he had gotten the best of it. Evander, on the other hand, was not so lucky. His handlers sat him down on a stool and were tending to his considerable wounds. He was defeated emotionally and mentally. He lacked the strength to stand on steady legs. Nothing was official, however, until Michael Buffer read the scorecards. Riddick Bowe got down on his knees and bowed his head in prayer. He demonstrated the cross symbol in front of his chest, awaiting potentially the biggest news of his life. He got back on his feet and paced around the ring, clearly giddy about the impending announcement. Michal Buffer read the scorecards to the attending and viewing audience:

> "Ladies and gentlemen we go to the scorecards. Chuck Giampa scores the fight 115–112, Jerry Roth scores it 117–110, and Dolby Shirly scores it 117–110 for the winner by unamouis decision . . . and NEW, Heavyweight . . . champion of the world, RIDDICK Big Daddy BOWE!"

Riddick Bowe jumped about ten feet in the air, screaming with delight. He was so excited, he lost his balance, almost falling on the ground. He was picked up by Rock Newman and embraced by his entire camp. It was a watershed moment for both Riddick Bowe and Rock Newman.

**Riddick Bowe:** I wanted to cry. It was like having a baby. Outside of my children being born, that is the greatest moment of my life. The journey and the hard work to get there made it that much better. I had beaten the best fighter in the world. There was never another moment like that in my career.

Evander was not disgraced in defeat. Even though only one man could win, both fighters were elevated with their performance. Critics of Evander's status as a true heavyweight were silenced. Scribes skeptical of Bowe's ability to deliver on his talent were squashed.

**Larry Merchant:** The first fight was one of the best heavyweight fights I feel anytime, anywhere. Great intensity. Holyfield, in his prime as a heavyweight, Bowe as a very serious young challenger, bell-to-bell action. The tenth round in my mind, in my personal YouTube, was indelible because of what it said about Holyfield and how big and strong Riddick was. Riddick Bowe and Evander Holyfield silenced critics and elevated themselves that night. Very rarely does one fight define both men, but this night was one of those occurrences.

Mackie Shilstone: Riddick Bowe was in the best shape of his career that night, no question. It can it can be attributed to an awesome training regimen. From the 6:00 a.m. runs to the Maggot juice, everything came together that night. Evander was in the ring with a superior physical specimen.

Steve Farhood: Over the course of his entire career. Riddick Bowe was always very good. He registered some good wins and had serious talent. The night he fought Evander Holyfield, however, was different. That night, he was a great fighter. An all-time effort. He could have given anyone problems on that night.

Harold Lederman: Great action fight. Evander showed tremendous heart and so did Riddick. Riddick Bowe did an outstanding job using his advantages. His jab was sharp, and those right hands were crushing. All-time great fight.

Freddie Roach: The result of the first fight did not surprise me at all. Eddie Futch was my mentor, so I spent a lot of time around Riddick Bowe. I worked with him for a short time, but I don't think Rock Newman liked me too much so that didn't last. Even so, that time with Bowe told me what Evander found out that night. Riddick Bowe was the bigger, better fighter. I expected Riddick to win as decisively as he did.

Richard Steele: Riddick was amazing in that fight. A lot of credit goes to Riddick for proving everyone wrong. Eddie Futch should get a lot credit as well.

Kieran Mulvaney: Truth be told, I don't think Evander Holyfield was regarded as an especially accomplished heavyweight champion at the time he signed to fight Riddick Bowe. I think he gained more in stature while losing that first bout than he had done in winning his other major bouts at heavyweight. Yes, he beat the man who beat the man, knocking out Buster Douglas in three in Las Vegas. But the Douglas he beat was a blubbery behemoth compared to the one who vanquished Mike Tyson on that famous night in Tokyo. And his reign since then had been unimpressive, taken the distance by veterans George Foreman and Larry Holmes and rocked by Bert Cooper. Yes, he was heavyweight champ, but it was hard for many to accept that he was anything other than a bulked-up cruiserweight. The reign would surely end once he faced a young skilled big heavyweight. Riddick Bowe was all those things, and he did end Holyfield's reign, but what a fight. Bowe just kept coming and coming, but Holyfield would not go away, constantly rallying, constantly fighting back. That first fight was one of the all-time great heavyweight title fights. And the tenth was one of the all-time great rounds in those all-time great heavyweight bouts. It looked like the world was Bowe's oyster after that. He had it all: a nice smile, an engaging personality, and boy, could he ever fight. But he could eat too, and his lack of conditioning made it a short ride at the top. Amazingly, the Holyfield fights wound up taking more out of Bowe than Holyfield. Twenty years later, Holyfield is the one fighting on, and Bowe has been out of the ring, with the odd exception, for fifteen years. Who would have thought? But on that one night against Holyfield, he was on top of the world.

Evander Holyfield spoke of retirement in the wake of the loss. At nearly thirty-four years old, the deposed champion alluded to possibly stepping away from the sport. He had come into the ring on top of the world. The boxing gods are a fickle bunch. Everything evolves when a title changes hands. It changes people's lives.

**Shelly Finkel:** **First fight was incredible. Evander wanted to retire, I told him to wait before announcing, and obviously he didn't listen.**

# 13
# Buggie Wuggie Wuggie

**R**iddick Bowe had defeated Evander Holyfield for the heavyweight title. After the fight, the two different dressing rooms were in stark contrast emotionally. In one dressing room, you had a brand-new heavyweight champion. In the other dressing room, you had a fallen warrior who was carried out on his shield. It had been a glorious night for boxing. After the post fight press conference, Evander Holyfield held his customary reception in the upper reaches of the hotel and casino.

Kathy Duva: After all of Evander's fights, he would always have a party celebrating victory. Since he had lost, this was not exactly a celebration. I would liken it to a wake. Evander still elected to have the party anyways because that's how he was. He is quite a jovial individual even in the face of defeat. Evander used to do the electric slide at these parties, and everyone would get up with him and dance when the DJ played that song. Evander loved to dance, and he wanted everyone in the room to know how good he was. I remember that night, Evander walked into the room looking all busted up. The second he walked in they, played the electric slide. Evander started dancing and everyone joined him. It was an emotional moment. Very emotional. We all loved him so much. I slipped out for a second to go to the bathroom and ran into Riddick. Riddick was such a sweet guy; he asked me if Evander was OK. I motioned for him to follow me down the hall, and when I opened the door to the party, there was Evander doing the electric slide, laughing and having a good time. The look on Riddick's face when he saw Evander was worth a million dollars. It was cute that Riddick was worried about him. That was proof to me that the fight would not affect their friendship.

Riddick Bowe would have quite a championship night. He partied and danced until the sun came up. He courted multiple women and popped the bubbly. He had earned every second of it. The coronation of a king is always fun to watch in any walk of life; it's the beginning of an era and the end of another. Evander Holyfield had come into the fight at the height of his powers and superstardom. He left the fight a beaten man who was beltless. Riddick Bowe's name had been etched in the same American granite as Jack Dempsey and James Braddock. The undisputed heavyweight championship of the world is very much a political office. An office with infinite international jurisdiction. He would be star not just in America, but the seven seas over. It's quite an extraordinary transformation. Riddick Bowe's personality would also add to his star power. Many who have interacted with him took a liking to his gentle giant persona; they knew that it would supplement his fame.

**Lou Dibella:** I always liked Riddick. I have had a relationship going back many years with him. He was good kid. I was close to him and I know for a fact what a good guy he was to those around him. Heck, he was at my wedding in 1992. We were both New York guys, so there was a lot of common ground. In my time at HBO, he was one of my favorite fighters easily.

**Marc Ratner:** I have vivid memories of Riddick doing Ali impersonations, and he could really do them well. He was very personable and friendly, very much like an overgrown kid. He was a very playful guy. Always had a smile on his face.

**Kathy Duva:** A very sweet, personable guy. I had known Riddick way before we ever put Holyfield in with him. He used to workout with my father-in-law's camp for a short time. Everyone liked him, very friendly guy. Lou had to kick him out of camp because he was being lazy, but it certainly had nothing to do with his personality.

**Larry Merchant:** I enjoyed being around him. He was a very bright kid, he was funny, he was a New York guy, and he had a certain wit. His jolly giant manner made him popular among boxing people

**George Ward:** A nice, honest guy. Every time I saw him, he had a smile on his face. He never gave me an ounce of trouble and was one of the few genuine fighters that I worked with. I have seen some bad people in the sport of boxing, and Riddick is the farthest thing from it

Riddick Bowe was in the driver's seat to achieve fame and financial success beyond his wildest dreams. Beyond anyone's wildest dreams. Everything seemed to be in front of him. Dan Duva and Rock Newman were in talks with the Chinese empire to stage a heavyweight fight against George Foreman. The projected purse would be gigantic. Before Riddick could move toward making that fight, an old friend became a mitigating factor. The first roadblock would be a political one. In defeating Razor Ruddock in a sensational fashion, Lennox Lewis had become Riddick Bowe's mandatory. Lennox's merit was not just limited to sanctioning bodies. The public and the media believed it was the best heavyweight fight that could be made. In the wake of his victory, Riddick Bowe had been appointed the best heavyweight in the world. Now he would have to prove it. Or so everyone thought.

# 14

# Lennox

Lennox Lewis and Riddick Bowe were not strangers .In 1988 at the Seoul Olympics, Lewis had defeated Bowe on a technicality to seize the gold medal and deny Bowe the clout he needed to ensure a lucrative promotional contract. The major promoters claim to this day that Bowe's emotional disposition was the reason they did not sign him. That's bullshit. It was because Bowe did not win the gold medal. Bowe is duly aware of this.

**Riddick Bowe:** I could not sniff a promotional contract when I came out. There is no doubt in my mind that I get a million off the top if I win that fight in Korea. I could have come home, been on the Wheaties box, all that. That's what makes the job that Rock Newman did so impressive. I may have lost to Lennox Lewis, but I was world champion before Lennox. I was making more money than he was. I guess it was fate, you know.

Lewis had won the fight in a strange fashion; the conclusion of the fight raised many questions. Questions that would follow Riddick until he lifted the heavyweight title from Evander Holyfield. One of the questions that still lingered, despite the title victory, stemmed from his days as an Olympian. Could he defeat Lennox Lewis? Lennox didn't think so. Lewis showed no shame in letting the world know this much. Lennox Lewis sent Bowe's career on a mini tailspin after the Olympics, and here he was, primed to do it yet again

Lennox Lewis, for all intents and purposes, stalled the progression of Bowe's boxing career. He cost him untold millions in endorsement deals, even more money in network contracts. Lennox Lewis was a bit uncouth about the whole situation. If Lewis had been gracious in victory, and had not disrespected Bowe time and time again over those formative years, it is exponentially more likely that a fight between the two could have been arranged. Lewis's behavior was even more curious given an encounter that allegedly took place between the two men in a shower room.

**Riddick Bowe: I don't want to get into details but I had to tell to him I don't get down like that.**

It has circulated in some boxing circles and Brittish tabloids, that Lennox Lewis has led a private gay lifestyle at some point. Questions about Lennox's sexuality had actually begun in the United Kingdom. The media took notice of the lack of women that seem to surround the superstar. There had also been rumors flying around mother England that Lennox had "Shagged" Sol Campbell. An English footballer. If that is the case. That is his right. Lennox and his rumored lifestyle has never been confirmed by one independent source, but it has been said. Riddick Bowe's assertions(of which I will not print) are just allegations, but even allegations can be damaging. Lennox is quite lucky that Bowe opted for reticence instead of exposing his allegations and severely damaging Lennox's image at a time when being homosexual was not as accepted as it is today. Certainly not in a tough-guy sport like boxing. The disrespect would continue the second Bowe won the heavyweight title. The night Bowe defeated Holyfield; Lennox was ringside, providing analysis for a PPV carrier carrying the fight. Bowe stepped down from the ring, soaking in the greatest moment in his life, when he ran headfirst into Lennox Lewis. Cameras caught the scene; HBO ran with it, delaying Riddick Bowe's postfight interview. Lewis did not congratulate Bowe. He did not tip his cap. Lennox opted to inject himself into a glorious night by standing in Bowe's way, forcing a confrontation. The two exchanged heated words, and it appeared for a short time that a second heavyweight fight would take place at the Thomas and Mack Center. Cooler heads prevailed, but Lennox Lewis's arrogance made a bad impression on Riddick.

**Riddick Bowe: I wanted to knock him the fuck out. Right there, ringside, in front of everybody. How is the man not going to give me my respect after such a great performance? Dude is an asshole dog straight up.**

The WBC mandated that Bowe defend his version of the heavyweight title against Lennox Lewis within one hundred days or be stripped. Bowe, at this point, was swimming in money from his title victory and endorsement endeavors. Riddick Bowe did not desperately need Lennox Lewis. Rock and Bowe would try to make the fight, but they would not go too far out of their way to do so. If Lennox had kept his mouth shut and not been so disrespectful of Bowe, maybe Rock would have gone into talks with a more understanding attitude. HBO also had a say in this thing along with the WBC. Originally, HBO wanted the Lewis-Ruddock and Holyfield-Bowe fights to be a final four of sorts. Three of the fighters had agreed to the setup contractually. Riddick Bowe was the only one that did not sign the contract. In the wake of his victory over Holyfield, Riddick Bowe and Lennox Lewis were reportedly offered a thirty-million dollar purse to which they could negotiate the split. Rock Newman, according to reports, offered Lennox Lewis a 90–10 split of the purse that HBO had allegedly put on the table. From a business standpoint alone, that was insane. If that is true, it's a very unreasonable offer that Lennox Lewis and Frank Maloney had every right to pass on. Lennox Lewis had not yet burst onto the American scene, but he was a huge draw in England. Lennox had also snuffed Razor Ruddock in two rounds. Yes, Lennox Lewis was not yet a star in America, but he was a star overseas. Rock's contention seemed to be that Riddick Bowe was the much bigger star and didn't need Lennox Lewis. The low-ball offers, however, made it seem like Bowe didn't want the fight. Rock had even been quoted as saying that it "was not financially sound to fight Lennox Lewis right away". To many it did not seem like an economical issue. The issue seemed to be that Rock Newman was steering clear of Lennox Lewis. Rock Newman gave Frank Maloney two options after the first round of negociations, fight Riddick Bowe now for three million, or wait a year, and fight him next fall for nine million. That offer was rejected as it should have been. The two sides went back and forth about what Lennox's cut should be. Lennox Lewis share of the profit was a consistent problem. A heavy sticking point, that no one talks about, is Dan Duva. Dan Duva was due 28 percent of Riddick Bowe based on the agreement that was reached prior to the first Holyfield fight. Dan Duva also had secured promotional rights to Lennox Lewis. Dan Duva was a major figure in the Bowe/Lewis negociation. Dan was due x amount of dollars when the fight was staged, that had to be accounted for at all times by both sides. Dan Duva stood to pocket a piece of every dollar that came in. Dan Duva had displayed foresight in securing crucial options on Riddick Bowe before the Holyfield fight. Those options were now costing Riddick major dollars. They were also giving Rock Newman all he could handle. Dan Duva was running the show. Rock Newman and Frank Maloney were managers, Dan Duva was the promoter. As explained before, the promoter cast a long shadow over everything. Especially when the promoter is due considerable points from each side. Managers only have so much power contractually. Frank Maloney and Lennox Lewis were asking for a ten million dollar guarantee. So Rock Newman would have to split the purse amogest 4 parties. Himself, Riddick Bowe, Lennonx Lewis, and Dan Duva. HBO would want their cut in some capacity as well. That is a difficult equation to balance. The fight on the surface appeared to be lucrative, but if you factor in the hands in the pot, it really wasn't. Not for Rock Newman and Riddick Bowe. At first, Rock attempted to cut down on Duva's share at which point Duva told him "I am not paying your bills". "Rock Newman is asking Dan to give up his options" Main Events spokeswoman Kathy Duva said at the time. Rock Newman was in a tough spot. After some internal discussions, it was decided that Lennox Lewis was literally more trouble than he was worth. Passing on the fight was deemed the prudent course of action. Rock Newman informed the WBC that Bowe would vacate the title, and so began the uproar.

Championship belts meant a lot more to the heavyweight division back in the early '90s than they do now. That could be because there were only three major titles back then as opposed to four now, five if you count the IBO which this writer does not. One fact has remained true through both eras and all of boxing history. The lineal championship is more important than any single belt or magazine/Internet ranking. The man to beat the man supersedes all claims to the championship of a given division. Today, *Ring* magazine champions are considered to be the lineal kingpin of their respective division. *Ring* magazine (because of its business relationship with an active promoter) unto itself is flawed; the only true way is the man who beat the man. Riddick Bowe at this point was the lineal heavyweight champion of the world. He had defeated Evander Holyfield who had defeated Buster Douglas who defeated Mike Tyson who defeated Michael Spinks who defeated Larry Holmes who defeated Ali/Spinks/Ali who defeated George Foreman who defeated Joe Frazier who defeated Cassius Clay who defeated Sonny Liston who defeated Floyd Patterson and so on and so forth. The WBC title, as lavish as it looked, was not necessary for Bowe to claim he was the heavyweight champion of the world. As talented and deserving as Lennox Lewis was, he was not necessary for Bowe to make a hefty paycheck. It would be a good PR move to appease boxing critics; to Bowe's camp, however, it was seen as just another option. All of these factors, combined with the personal history, led Bowe to make a decision that many would hold against him and his legacy.

Lou DiBella: Not fighting Lennox Lewis hurt him. It hurt him then and it still hurts him now. I believe many would see him in a different light if he had taken that fight. We at HBO pushed for it, but it was not to be.

Lem Satterfield: I do not think that, at the time, he was ducking him. It was a political issue. It was not as cut-and-dry as getting in the ring and fighting. There was more to the situation than that. But because Lewis had beaten Bowe as an amateur, and Lewis stopped Ruddock in the first round in October of 1992 after Ruddock had gone life-and-death with Tyson, it appeared that Bowe was avoiding him. Bowe was so good and so proud that I believe he and Rock Newman felt that they simply should not be dictated to. Some may believe Bowe to have feared Lewis. Maybe he did, later, but I do not believe that that was the case at the time. I believe that at the time, because he had Eddie Futch and because his skills were so great, that he would have gotten up for and beaten Lewis.

Thell Torrence: The truth is Riddick Bowe would have handled Lennox Lewis. At the time we wanted the fight because we knew we could win it. Lennox Lewis had touble with the jab. I remember when he attempted to hire us to train him; he asked us if we could help him with defending the jab. Right there in his kitchen, he told me to my face that was his weakness, and could we help him with it. The jab was one of Riddick Bowe's strengths. He would have beaten Lennox Lewis rather easily. This was before Lennox started working with Emanuel Steward. Prior to the adjustments that Steward made, Riddick Bowe would have defeated Lennox Lewis. No doubt about it.

In December 1992, Riddick Bowe and Rock Newman flew to London England to humiliate Lennox Lewis. Roughly a month after winning the title, Riddick Bowe called a press conference and tossed the WBC heavyweight title in the trash. He didn't do it alone. Rock Newman stood next to him and helped guide the belt into the trash. Bowe sought to show everyone that Lennox Lewis could come get his belt out of the trash. Riddick Bowe also wanted to show the world that he refused to hold a title he believed was secretly controlled by Don King. Riddick Bowe told the media, if Lennox Lewis vacated the title that was bestowed upon him, he would fight Lennox Lewis. A suspicion in Bowe's camp was that the WBC champion would be dictated to by Don King All of these factors, The WBC, Dan Duva, Lennox Lewis and his extravagant demands, was enough to make Rock Newman pass on the whole situation completely. Riddick Bowe did not really foresee the depth of the reaction that followed. Bowe saw the dumping of the belt as comical. No different than a professional wrestling gag. Fans, writers, and even boxing constituents saw it another way. They saw the situation as Riddick Bowe ducking Lennox Lewis. This is the prevailing opinion on the subject amongst media members and boxing fans alike. It is, and has been the subject of intense debate. What most fans fail to appreciate, and some writers too, is that Riddick Bowe did not need the risk or the stipulations that involved Lennox Lewis. Riddick Bowe made a public relations mistake, being so cavalier about giving the belt up. Staging a cause célèbre of a press conference was over-the-top. It was not necessary to cheapen the history of the heavyweight championship by throwing the belt in the trash.

**Riddick Bowe: I was following the advice of my handlers. I would have fought Lennox Lewis. Who the fuck was Len-**

nox Lewis, dog? I did not fear that man at all. I was told by people that I trust that I didn't need that fight. I did what I did because I was advised to do so.

Jim Lampley: Lennox Lewis was the more mature fighter from the beginning. Going back to Korea, Lennox always seemed to have the edge. If Riddick had been convinced that he had evolved enough as a professional to win, the fight would have happened. If a big hitter whacks another big hitter once, it's hard to regain your confidence. Some people thought that after Seoul, Riddick never truly believed he could beat Lewis. I have heard rumors that Lennox's name was on the contract, but Riddick would not sign. I have come to the conclusion that as a broadcast journalist, I am always going to piss someone off. When Riddick would talk to me, he would always bust my chops about complimenting Lennox Lewis. He didn't like it. I would always tell him to prove me wrong if it bothered him that much. He never did.

Thom Loverro: I remember Larry Merchant saying after the first Bowe-Holyfield fight that it would be the time then to fight Lewis, because sometimes in boxing, these fights that you figure will get made never do for many unpredictable reasons. I think Rock Newman was smart to allow Bowe to establish himself as a heavyweight champion before facing Lewis (I also think Bowe won the rematch with Holyfield and was robbed of the decision). I suspect he and Lewis were close to a fight. Oliver McCall then knocked out Lewis.

Angelou Dundee: I believe that it is hard to discard a fighter simply because he did not win the gold. It did not stop Riddick from becoming heavyweight champion before the man who won the gold medal in 1988, Lennox Lewis. The key in that loss for Bowe following the Olympics was to not let it define him, and he didn't.

Ross Greenburg: First of all, the rumors of a thirty-million-dollar purse are false. I remember being at the Jesse Ferguson fight in Washington DC and thinking to myself, why is this not the Lennox Lewis fight? HBO made several offers to Rock Newman and Riddick Bowe to fight Lennox Lewis over a period of time. They didn't want the fight. I won't say they ducked the fight, but you do the math. Riddick Bowe, instead of fighting Lennox Lewis, got several consecutive soft touches from our network. That is a credit to Rock Newman. He was a master negotiator for Riddick Bowe. They were content to take the money and literally run from Lennox Lewis.

Kieran Mulvaney: I wasn't yet covering boxing back when Riddick Bowe was champion. Tell you the truth, I didn't even consider it likely. I was living in Amsterdam at the time, obliged, as most folks in Europe were in those pre-Internet days, to find out my boxing news a couple of months late, courtesy of *Ring* magazines that I would read in the newsagents without ever actually, you know, buying them. But, with the benefit of hindsight, the heavyweight championship at the time was an interesting situation with a real rivalry between some seriously gifted fighters—and, being British, I paid particular attention to it because of the emergence of Lennox Lewis. I remember thinking at the time that Lewis was going to prove to be something a bit special. I remember reading about him destroying Derek Williams and Glenn McCrory, and I watched live when he fairly easily handled Gary Mason. And then of course came the destruction of Razor Ruddock in a fight that even the British hacks picked him to lose, largely on the basis of Ruddock's strong showings in back-to-back fights against Mike Tyson. With Ruddock out the way, there was nothing to stop him fighting the winner of the Riddick Bowe-Evander Holyfield fight. Alas, no. Despite the sighs from boxing fans that the best don't fight the best anymore, by and large that isn't true. Most of the big fights do get made, albeit sometimes only eventually. Heck, Mike Tyson finally got around to fighting Evander Holyfield, even though the first attempt to make the fight failed when he went to jail. But the failure of Bowe to fight Lewis stands tall in the pantheon of great fights that didn't happen. And to this day, I still don't fully understand why. I know now, which I did not then, that there was an offer on the table from HBO, but that Bowe and Rock Newman reportedly wanted a 90-10 split—which is, of course, tantamount to saying they didn't want the fight. Were they just trying to gain psychological one-upmanship, belittling Lewis and Union-Flag-jacket-wearing Frank Maloney? You have to think it was, as was the decision to throw the WBC belt in the trash. Team Bowe wanted, I think, to convey that they were bigger than Lewis, too big to be forced to fight anyone. Unfortunately, instead the image it conveyed was that he just didn't want any part of the Brit, particularly given that Lewis had stopped Bowe in the Olympic final. But the thing of it is Bowe would have been a big favorite in that fight; you have to think that, at that stage in their relative professional development, he would have wiped the canvas with Lewis. The Ruddock win aside, Lewis didn't have any signature wins against truly world-class talent; he wound up struggling against Frank Bruno of all people. He didn't even look so great against Phil Jackson or Tony Tucker. By the time discussions about a Bowe-Lewis fight began to warm up again, Riddick had lost the Fan Man fight and Lewis was crumbling under the might of the legendary Oliver McCall. Bowe had missed his chance, one that would surely have set him up to be viewed far more favorably by history than he is.

The dumping of the belt added to public and private perception that Bowe ducked Lewis. Because many saw Bowe's behavior as immature and self-absorbed, they were much more comfortable indicting Bowe as a ducker. It's an understandable position. Lennox Lewis would go on to be knocked out by Oliver McCall at the scene of his third title defense in one of the bigger upsets in boxing history. The sight of Lennox Lewis stumbling about the ring, begging the referee for mercy, at the very least, was enjoyable for Riddick Bowe.

**Riddick Bowe:** Good, I was laughing my ass off watching Lewis get knocked out by a bum. How could he have competed with me? He could not even whup Oliver McCall. On top of that, he was being dictated to by Don King. Can't say I felt sorry for him.

As 1992 came to a close, Riddick Bowe soaked in the greatest year of his life. He was heavyweight champion. He had silenced the Ferdie Pacheco's, the so-called experts that had questioned his heart and credibility. He had proven to the world that he was the genuine article. Manifest destiny had driven him to greatness, and this feat, this achievement, would live forever. Riddick had done some damage at the box office as well. The only person who made more money than Riddick Bowe in 1992 was Michael Jordan. Bowe was set for life financially, or so it would seem. The challenge now was to mow down every enemy in his path and take his place in the pantheon amongst the pound-for-pound boxers of the era.

# 15
# Juicy

Riddick Bowe was rich. Riddick Bowe had climbed the heavyweight mountain and annexed it. His reign atop the division began in February 1993, staging a homecoming in Madison Square Garden.

The business of boxing has many facets, among them is the homecoming. When a fighter wins a title or registers a meaningful progression, it is commonplace to capitalize on the notoriety that accompanies such a victory. Staging a homecoming is typically an easy way to cash in. It is also common for a fighter to come home after a tough defeat. A homecoming fight is like a pep rally for the headline attraction. Team Bowe knew that they would have to come home at some point and did so immediately. It was only natural to do it in the wake of his heavyweight championship victory. New York City likes winners, and they like winners from New York even more. New York City supported Riddick Bowe, packing Madison Square Garden fight night. Riddick Bowe defended his WBA and IBF heavyweight titles against Michael Dokes on February 3, 1993. Riddick Bowe would disappoint his fans, stopping an overmatched Michael Dokes in the very first round of the fight. The fight appeared to still be a contest when it was called. Riddick Bowe landed tremendous power punches, but Michael Dokes did not touch the canvas. He was knocked down, but it was a technicality. Dokes fell into the ropes at one point, but they appeared to hold him up. In boxing, if the ropes keep you on your feet, it is scored a knockdown. A stunned Dokes took the standing eight count. Riddick Bowe, sensing the end was near, placed his punches perfectly and reduced Dokes to a hapless old man stumbling around the ring. The stoppage, however, was perceived as abrupt and slightly premature. Riddick Bowe was actually booed by his fans as the official decision was announced. It was a disgraceful act by the fight fans of New York City. The fans of New York City have not had an undisputed heavyweight champion since, which unto itself serves some justice for Riddick Bowe. Riddick had chosen to honor his New York lineage, as opposed to a much more lucrative fight with George Foreman. The appreciation he received was despicable. The crowd was about as lively as a tardy Lakers crowd before the questionable ending. Something else could have contributed to the subdued nature of the crowd. The wonderful social monarch, Arthur Ashe, had died the night of the fight, and when his death was relayed, it surprised many at ringside. Maybe that contributed, but it does not excuse booing a young hometown heavyweight champion. He knocked out a lesser fighter early, and for that he should be showered with boos? Any astute fight fan attending the fight could not have thought Dokes was a live dog. The knockout was a formality. And it was a knockout. It's not like the champion lumbered to a dull decision. In a stroke of irony, Michael Dokes suffered the same type of quick stoppage that he had enjoyed several years earlier when he lifted the WBA heavyweight title from "Muscular" Mike Weaver in 1982. As the crowd booed and the HBO commentators complained, one thing became clear, Now that Riddick Bowe was heavyweight champion, he would be expected to perform like one.

Rock Newman had big plans for Riddick Bowe. Rock saw potential in Riddick Bowe in the ring and at the box office. Riddick Bowe, in his heart, wanted to be the next Ali. Rock played to that to some degree. He wanted Riddick's influence to transcend boxing. To be a poor man's John Lennon. To touch the lives of people all over the planet with his platform. There were massive amounts of money to be made in representing a young personable heavyweight champion. Rock Newman did what anyone in business does, he attempted to maximize the situation. Rock Newman would go about squeezing all the juice out of the orange and, along the way, made a decision that caused quite a stir in boxing circles.

After showcasing Riddick throughout the continental United States, Rock opted to take Riddick Bowe on a worldwide tour in effort to add a social touch to Riddick's newfound fame. The tour would feature dignitaries from all cultures and countries. Riddick Bowe rubbed elbows with Nelson Mandela, had an audience with the pope, and comforted the sick and dying in Africa. The duration of the tour was not in infinite, two weeks, but it did take its toll. A fighter's body is his temple, and constant travel without rest is not really ideal. Riddick was less than a month removed from fighting Dokes and was scheduled to fight again in May.

**Riddick Bowe:** We went everywhere. There was not a lot of time to rest. I had a good time and met so many people, but it took me out of the gym. I started to eat more than I would have if I had been home. Rock was my manager; he had gotten me to the top of the world at that point, so I was not going to question him. If I could do the whole thing over, I would not have gone. The tour set me back. It was a good marketing decision, but it was not a good boxing decision. No two ways about it, that world tour hurt me physically.

Rock Newman was very busy. He filed a lawsuit in New York City District Court against Main Events Inc. Evander Holyfield and Shelly Finkel were named in suit. The twenty-four-page civil complaint made several sensational allegations. Spencer Promotions and Main Events had entered into an agreement when they made the first Holyfield-Bowe fight. Rock Newman, through court documents, charged that Main Events was involved in a conspiracy with concerned sanctioning bodies to force Riddick Bowe to vacate his belts. Rock Newman believed that Riddick Bowe could have made an eight-figure pay-day to fight heavyweight contender Tommy Morrison, but because of the alleged machinations of Main Events, that was made impossible. Specific charges ranged from breach of fiduciary responsibility to interference with prospective economic advantage. The complaint also charged Main Events with breach of contract. Rock Newman was seeking twenty-five-million dollars in retribution. Rock Newman denounced his copromoters. Telling the public that Dan Duva was doing everything he could to undermine Riddick Bowe's earning potential. Rock Newman cited a "conflict of interest" as his specific reasoning for filing the complaint. When informed of the suit, Dan Duva told a reporter, "That's all? Why not more?" One has to wonder the point of such a civil action. With an impending Holyfield rematch, the ongoing stipulations between the two parties, it made little sense to live in court and live with each other at the same time.

Rock Newman himself would not be above the law. He was charged in April of 1993 with battery, along with Bernard Brooks, a member of Bowe's entourage. Rock and Benard allegedly had a physical confrontation with a news photographer. Civil and criminal charges had been filed.

The photographer's name was Douglas Pizac. Douglas claimed that he climbed into the ring after the Riddick Bowe-Evander Holyfield fight, he was then assaulted. Douglas's injuries were considerable. Facial cuts requiring twelve stitches and an eye swollen shut. Rock Newman pled guilty to lesser charges and agreed to attend ten hours of "impulse control counseling." The codefendants were also ordered to pay a $1,000 fine.

To some, it seemed that between the assault, the lawsuit, and the world tour, Rock Newman was creating a lot of out-of-ring distractions for the brand-new champion. An impressionable twenty-five-year-old kid did not need so much drama at that point in his development. Rock Newman did not look for drama, but it did seem to follow him, and that was a dynamic that contributed to the circuslike atmosphere that seemed to be Bowe's camp. Rock Newman, in his heart, felt he was doing everything he could for Riddick Bowe. He believed in Bowe, loved Bowe, and wanted to make him an all-time great. Sometimes in that pursuit, however, he could be shortsighted and impulsive. Not to mention disagreeable.

**Larry Merchant:** Rock was a character, an advocate for his guy and so forth. Rock Newman had this vision of turning Riddick Bowe into the next Ali, a worldwide figure. Took him on a world tour, took him to Africa, all sorts of things. At the time, it may have seemed like a good marketing idea. This dynamic, among other things, may have contributed in some way to the short and happy career of Riddick Bowe as heavyweight champion. What Ali had, you cannot contrive that, you cannot make that up, it has to come from within, and there is only one Ali. Rock thought that Bowe could follow that path in a deliberate way, it may have seemed smart, but it did not turn out well. Who knows how it may have contributed, we don't know that.

**Angelou Dundee:** There will never be another Ali. Never. Riddick Bowe himself wanted to be the next Ali. Rock Newman was attempting to help Bowe reach that dream.It was nothing more than a manager attempting to publicize his fighter and make him a star.

Thell Torrence: From my perspective, the success of Riddick Bowe's career was the result of the aggressive marketing of Rock Newman. He got the most of him that anyone could have. He did an excellent job. He respected me, he fought with the media, he fought with people around him. He did it all with one objective in mind. He was smart enough to know what he had. He did a great job. At that time, we didn't get involved with the business side too much. He was in charge, he was dealing with the media, and he felt he had the best fighter in the world. No matter what anyone thinks, Rock thought he could beat anyone in the world, There were some fights I disagreed with, but I give him credit, he would come to me and ask my opinion on some fights. He had a feel for what was going on at all times within the camp. Some managers don't really have their hand on the pulse of a camp. Rock Newman was not one of those guys.

Rock Newman had also become a power broker, and his influence was not limited to boxing. He organized relief efforts in Africa. Rock helped the disgraced DC Mayor Marion Barry take back public office when he was released from prison. He rubbed elbows with Bill Clinton. Rock Newman was a social activist. He truly cared for the advancement of African Americans and campaigned to that effect. Rock Newman should be commended for his efforts to help the black community. The problem was that Rock was a little too focused on Rock. The perception to some was that Rock Newman was using Riddick Bowe in ring exploits to further his social agenda. "The world tour was more about Rock Newman than Riddick Bowe," a boxing insider said. Rock Newman did right by Riddick Bowe on the financial front. Making history, Rock Newman negotiated a six-fight deal with HBO and Caesars Palace that would pay Riddick Bowe in excess of one hundred million dollars should he continue winning. It was the biggest media contract given to a prizefighter ever in the history of the sport. No lucky charms at the end of this rainbow, just barrels and barrels of cash. Riddick Bowe was rich beyond his wildest dreams.

**Riddick Bowe:** That contract was straight. One hundred million is a lot of money dog. Rock and I have had our differences, but that was one situation that he got right. That money seemed to set me for life. Rock saw a percentage, but at the end of the day, that deal made me rich, and I will always appreciate that.

Rock Newman cut another landmark deal in the spring of 1993. Riddick Bowe was an HBO fighter; however, Rock Newman had given Bowe the wiggle room contractually to sign with international carriers. Rock Newman capitalized on this piece of fine print. Rock Newman and Riddick Bowe agreed to allow a British TV carrier to televise his next five fights, beginning with a taped delayed broadcast of his fight with Michael Dokes. The United Kingdom's Independent Television (ITV or as it is known today "Channel 3") provided English fight fans a chance to see the reigning heavyweight champion. ITV, outside of being a direct competitor with the BBC, is the oldest television network in England. Very much like a CBS or an NBC. Specific numbers were not released, but the bottom line was rumored to be in the millions. According to sources in the United Kingdom, this contract was a preemptive strike by Independent Television. Lennox Lewis and Riddick Bowe seemed like they were on a collision course. In the event that the fight came off, the network wanted to make sure they would carry the fight. Independent Television, in effect, headed BBC and Sky Sports off at the pass. Even though the fight never came off, the contract was a surefire sign that Riddick was becoming a worldwide figure. As Riddick's public profile continued to expand, the task of managing the emerging mogul would require proper administration.

Rock Newman had recently started Spencer Promotions to give some structure to the promoting of the new champion. Spencer Promotions would handle all things for Riddick for the rest of his career. The HBO contract, however, was not a sure thing; it was drawn up under the assumption of continued success.

**Lou Dibella:** The contract was predicated upon winning. It's not like we offered him the money up front. He had to earn it. There really is no boxing contract that is not based on winning

A source of money not predicated upon victory was endorsements. Fruit of the Loom began running national commercials featuring the new champion. International juggernaut, Fila, created an entire line of clothing named "Bowe Motion." Nintendo got in on the act, agreeing to develop a video game named after the champ. Riddick Bowe ran the talk show gamut and was beginning to tap mainstream America. Rock Newman, was at the center of the booming Riddick Bowe industry. Every deal, every negotiation, every payoff was the result of the tireless work of Rock Newman to market his product.

Riddick Bowe went on tour for about two weeks after the Dokes fight. He then took an optional against Jesse Ferguson in his adopted hometown of Washington DC. Jesse Ferguson was a long shot in every sense of the word. The plan had been for Riddick to fight Ray Mercer in his next fight, but Mercer had been upset by Ferguson the night Riddick Bowe took out Michael Dokes. A cruel subplot within the promotion was that Jesse would only be completely compensated if he made it through the end of the first round. Jesse had no business in the ring with Riddick Bowe. He had gotten a little lucky against Ray Mercer and was not a true threat to the heavyweight championship. The matchmaking had recently been an Achilles' heel for Bowe's image, and here it was again, reeling its ugly head. The HBO-televised main event was an unnecessaryshowcase fight. Bowe had just dispensed with Dokes in one round, and fight fans were eager to see him involved in a fight with some danger attached to it. Jesse Fergueson was not game in any sense of the word. Before fans could get comfortable in their seats, Riddick Bowe blew Jesse Ferguson away in two rounds. Riddick landed power shots throughout the four minutes of the fight. It was an awesome display of offensive firepower but yet again left something to be desired to boxing pundits. Those close to Bowe felt this was Riddick Bowe's most dominant performance.

**Thell Torrence:** Eddie Futch told me after the fight that was the best Riddick has ever looked. Ever. That Riddick Bowe would have beaten any heavyweight in history. Big, strong, and technically sound. If we could have maintained that Riddick Bowe, who knows how far we would have gone.

**Ross Greenburg:** We paid a six-million-dollar license fee for that fight. Wow. For a soft touch that's a huge fee to pay. Again, that's a testament to Rock Newman. That fee is twice the amount we paid for Devon Alexander-Timothy Bradley. If you figure in inflation, wow, what a payday for zero resistance.

Riddick Bowe had been heavyweight champion for almost a year. He had traveled the world and defended his titles in his two hometowns of New York City and Washington DC. As Riddick Bowe's star continued to rise, his personal habits, and his dedication the sport, deteriorated at a geometric rate.

**Emanuel Steward:** Eddie Futch and I go back a long way. He is a Detroit guy. Eddie called me after the Ferguson fight and told me he had lost control of Riddick Bowe. He told me that Riddick was doing what he wanted, when he wanted. He lost control of Riddick, and no one seemed to be able to get Riddick to focus. Eddie told me he was living a totally undisciplined lifestyle outside of the ring.

Riddick Bowe picked a pretty inopportune time to lose focus. On the horizon, foaming at the mouth was a rejuvenated Evander Holyfield.

# Episode Two

Riddick Bowe's decline physically can be attributed to one undeniable fact. He was wildly reckless with his eating habits. Mackie Shilstone had been brought in to revolutionize Riddick's approach to his nutrition and conditioning. He temporarily achieved success, refurbishing Bowe's physical profile, and propelling him to the heavyweight championship. As with many situations in life, you can take someone to the river, but you can't force him or her to drink. Mackie dedicated endless amounts of time to keeping Bowe in fine tune physically. Those that blame Mackie Shilstone for Riddick Bowe's falling off the beaten path shortchanges the extraordinary work that Mackie did with Riddick in the time they were together. Mackie Shilstone did not work with Riddick after the first Holyfield fight; his absence hurt Riddick Bowe more than he realized at the time. After Bowe won the heavyweight title, he did what a lot of people do when they reach their respective goal. He enjoyed the spoils; he began to train a little less and eat a little more. Slowly beneath his nose, the seeds for a fall were being planted. Riddick's behavior was not encouraged by his camp, but it was not controlled either. Mackie Shilstone had been ousted after the first Holyfield fight; the effects of such a decision would be ever reaching. Riddick Bowes diet was not monitored like it should have been. Eddie Futch's job was to train Riddick Bowe, not babysit him. Where was Rock Newman in all of this? Rock Newman should get 100 percent credit for Riddick's rise; it is only natural to assign him some blame for Riddick's physical drop-off. If Rock had spent as much time correcting Riddick's bad habits, as he did on the DC political scene, Riddick Bowe's title reign would have lasted a little longer than it did. The glamorous world tour, the lack of discipline, and a propensity to spend money like a sultan turned Riddick Bowe's camp into a train wreck in the lead up to the second Holyfield fight. Where was Jesse Jackson? Jesse Jackson had a habit, when Americans were actually competitive in the heavyweight division, of being a "close confidant" of whoever happens to be the heavyweight champion. Why didn't Jesse Jackson counsel

Riddick during those turbulent times? Jesse Jackson's presence in camp was of a self-serving nature, we all know that. He still could have used his considerable wisdom to guide the young champion.

Another colossal distraction in Bowe's life was the shady doings of the people that claimed to love him. Much like MC Hammer, Bowe spent endless amounts of money on everyone around him. When he won the title, the sharks got even busier. Cars, houses, clothes, shoes for over twenty people that did not do much in return. Riddick Bowe assumed people's entire livelihoods. Riddick Bowe made nothing short of a fortune. The people around him did everything possible to undermine that fact.

**Riddick Bowe:** **I was buying cars and houses for people that I never got to live in or drive. I would come home and money would be missing from my account. A lot of money. I also was constantly under pressure to donate money to a church that my wife attended in Washington DC. Every time I looked up, someone had his or her hand out. It was never ending, and I will admit it distracted me. My wife spent so much of my money that it bordered on criminal. She also was not asking me to do so. She was buying things for her family that I didn't even know about. I could not have had worse people around me at that point in time.**

The second fight with Evander Holyfield was inevitable. Rematches in boxing are as sure as the sun rising. There was no question in anyone's mind that the fight would be made eventually. It was the natural progression for both fighters at that point in time. Going into the second act, many figured that the story of the first fight would play out even more emphatically in the second go-round. There were some in the media that feared for Evander's well-being going into the second fight.

**Kathy Duva:** **I remember walking into the fight with my husband and seeing Jim Lampley shortly before the fight. He had a look of concern on his face. He asked us if we**

thought Evander could actually win the fight. He seemed genuinely concerned about Evander going in. It seemed we were the only ones that actually gave Evander a chance going in.

**Jim Lampley:** I thought that Bowe had done what bigger men do to smaller men by the end of the first fight. I figured the second fight would be a more decisive than the first time. I thought it would be a less-intense second version. That's what usually happens in a rematch. Emanuel has a way of seeing things from a different perspective. That's why he wins so many fights. He changed up, he created more movement. If you have ever seen Evander dance, it's pure vanity. He has to be the one that blows everyone away when he dances. Emanuel saw Evander dance in that nightclub and knew that was the key to beating Riddick Bowe. I will admit, going into the fight, I thought Riddick would do more damage than the first fight.

**Riddick Bowe:** I had not a good camp. I came in heavier than I would have liked. I was ready to fight mentally, but physically, I just didn't have it that night. I figured that Evander would try to stand up to me again, and I knew that there was no way he would be able to do that for twelve rounds and make it through the fight. That's what I figured. What actually happened is a different story.

# 17

# Fan Man

Act two of the eventual trilogy would be a little less action packed than the first tussle. The fight took place on November 6, 1993. Riddick Bowe, now the champion, would make a career-high purse of $5,000,000. Evander Holyfield was in the midst of a boxing reformation under the tutelage of Hall of Fame trainer Emanuel Steward. Steward is of the famed Kronk Boxing Gym in Detroit, Michigan. Emanuel had witnessed the first fight from afar and wanted Evander to employ different tactics. Emanuel was not crazy about the assignment of Riddick Bowe right off the bat, however.

Emanuel Steward: I was not totally on board with the situation. I had been working a corner at a championship fight in Mexico. I got a call from MC Hammer telling me that Evander wanted me to train him. I flew down to Atlanta with Hammer to meet Evander, and after meeting for about three hours, I agreed to work with Evander Holyfield. I was apprehensive about fighting Riddick Bowe. He was so talented and big. It was a dangerous fight to Evander's health. Riddick had beaten Evander into retirement the first time out. I had gone to the Jesse Ferguson fight, and Riddick Bowe looked amazing. He looked so good in that fight that I figured beating that Bowe may have been impossible. One night, Evander and I went out to a nightclub because we both like to dance. When I saw him dancing, I knew that was the key to beating Riddick Bowe. The whole camp, we focused on side-to-side movement. In and out, staying on our toes. We based the entire game plan on making Riddick twist and turn. It worked to perfection.

**Evander Holyfield:** Camp was great. I really employed the weights in that camp. Manny helped me with the strategy, and my conditioning team helped me expand my physical dimensions. I had heard stories that Bowe was distracted, the world tour and so forth. I knew that I was going to win the fight. While he is worried about this and that, I am worried about one thing. The title.

Evander had also gained a cool ten pounds of muscle since the first fight, in an effort to give himself a better chance to stand up to the physicality of the bigger champion. Evander was moving in and out, constantly giving Bowe all types of angles and feints. This threw Riddick off just enough to make the fight a completely different animal than the first fight. Riddick Bowe found himself chasing a sharp counterpuncher, which can be a recipe for disaster. Evander was landing clean punches, but not punches in bunches. He never really put combinations together. He was not interested in a knockout. He was concerned with piling up the points with crisp counterpunching. He intended to take his belt back in a twelve-round decision. Bowe was frustrated beyond belief, and his frustration was evident.

**Riddick Bowe:** He was staying out of harm's way. He was moving and dodging. He knew if he stood and fought, I would tap that ass. He came out fighting the right game plan, and it threw off my timing just a little bit.

As the fight passed the halfway point, it appeared that Evander Holyfield was well on his way to regaining the title. He was landing clean punches and seemed to be gathering momentum with each round. The fight was shaping up to be yet another defining moment in Holyfield's career. Before Evander could have his moment, however, someone else decided to have his. The electrifying arrival of James Miller, "Fan Man" could very well be the strangest, most chaotic moment in boxing history.

At 1:23 of the seventh round, Riddick Bowe and Evander Holyfield were knee-deep into their heavyweight championship fight when an unidentified man (at the time) flew into Caesars Palace on a parachute, landing on the ropes, and causing massive confusion and fear. He had been airborne for several minutes. HBO, ever cognizant, had caught the idiot on camera well before his arrival. This was not an accidental occurrence. James Miller had given himself control over his jump. A motor powered his parachute; this contraption emitted a loud buzzing sound as it approached the ring. The parachute got stuck in the lights as he landed, much to the horror of those at ringside. The scene was an unprecedented one in sports history. It was not much different from an entertainer flying into the halftime show of the Super Bowl. Jim Lampley's call of the landing for HBO is one that will live forever in boxing lore.

> **"Someone with a parachute has . . . landed on the edge of the ring, the fight has been stopped, there is a massive melee at ringside."**

Fan Man, in retrospect, could not have picked a more dangerous situation to descend into. Present ringside were four different entities that would take colossal exception to his flight. You had Caesars Palace security, they didn't really appreciate being embarrassed in front of a live HBO audience; you had the Fruit of Islam, the security detail for the Nation of Islam. They are world-famous for their dedication to protecting their leader. That leader, in this case, was Louis Farrakhan. You had Riddick Bowe's security, individuals that were not exactly beacons of light. You had the metro cops that govern Las Vegas itself. Fan Man did not really take into account the situation he was getting himself into from a personal point of view. Along with Louis Farrakhan at the fight was civil rights leader Jesse Jackson. The two men were prominent figures in Black America socially. The initial fear of many from ringside was that Fan Man's entrance was an elaborate attempt on their lives. Fan Man's entrance is an entertaining story, no matter the vessel.

**Ross Greenburg:** I remember we had a cameraman in a blimp or a helicopter that night. Our cameraman was doing what we call zoom shots from way above the stadium. He sent us a communication telling us, "Look at this!" I saw a man coming down from the heavens with some type of gadget and a parachute. It was simply bizarre. We saw him well before anyone else did. At first I wasn't sure if I wanted to show the shot on the telecast, it could embolden a lot of people to attempt what this loony tune was doing. I went back and forth with Mark in production, trying to figure out what to do about this. This was a news story developing that had nothing to do with boxing. When he landed, I was not surprised, shockingly. When I first saw the shots of him flying, I knew in the back of my mind him landing was a possibility, but we didn't anticipate it actually happening. I remember the Fruit of Islam and everyone else wearing him out when he landed. It was a truly strange situation.

Terry Lane: For years I had begged my dad to take me to Las Vegas with him. I begged and pleaded until my mother finally allowed me to accompany my father to a fight. What a first fight to go to. It was the Holyfield-Bowe rematch. It was a great fight even though Bowe lost. As everyone knows, it was the event that featured Fan Man. I actually saw him flying around the stadium, circling around before his final descent. I remember thinking to myself, "I am in Las Vegas, it is probably some type of side show." I thought initially it was part of the festivities. All of a sudden, I hear everybody booing. I was really high in the stands, this was back when they used to build makeshift stadiums outside for big fights. I was in the north part of the stadium. Fan Man actually flew into the ring from the side of the stadium that I was sitting in. So my view of the situation was unlike anything one person can imagine. He literally flew over my head down towards the ring. I then saw him land on the ring; no one knew what to make of it.

Marc Ratner: It was a strange weekend before Fan Man. I remember going to see Riddick Bowe the day before the fight. I got his suite information and headed up there to do some commission business. The Nation of Islam was guarding his door, these real big Nation of Islam guys, they were all at least six foot four, 250 pounds. I was lucky enough to be the one who had to bring the gloves to Riddick's room. I remember having to get permission just to go inside of his dressing room, and I am the head executive of the commission. It was an intense visit. The fight? Forget about it. What a fiasco. It certainly revolves around the Fan Man. The ironic thing about that, depending on where you were sitting, is that usually in a fight, if there happens to be a fight in the crowd or something going on outside in the ring, the crowd will generate a type of buzz that draws everyone's attention to whatever may be going on. I started to hear that sound, but I did not see anything right away. I was told later he circled around for a while. I did not actually see him until he was right on top of the ring. This was in 1993, so terrorism awareness was not what it is today. If it had been today, in these times, the scene may have been even crazier than it was. The Fan Man landed in Riddick's corner. Seated behind that corner at the time of his landing was civil rights leader Jesse Jackson and Minister Louis Farrakhan. My initial thoughts were that someone was after them. It was a fear that thank God was not confirmed. The scene was absolutely chaotic, but the person who deserves a lot of credit, and does not get it for keeping some semblance of order that night, is Michael Buffer. He did a tremendous job of keeping the crowd calm. He stayed on the microphone throughout the entire situation. That was a big because that situation could have developed into an all-time riot. I was not sure what to do. It's not as if there is a specific protocol to follow in the event that a man parachutes into the ring. In retrospect, I should have sent both guys back to the dressing room. At the time, we did not know how long the situation would last or what it would be, so I made the decision not to do that. If I had known that it would be a twenty-one-minute delay, I would have sent them back because it was a little cold that night; we ended up just putting blankets on them. The aspect of the situation that no one talks about is how much time was left in the round. I believe there was 1:21 that was left at the time of the stoppage in action. I remember going around to the three judges and reminding them to remember where they were at from a scoring point of view because we were going to score this round. If I remember correctly, one judge scored the round for Bowe, one scored it for Holyfield, and then one scored it even. If the judge who has scored that round even had given it to Bowe, I believe that Bowe would have been given a draw and kept his title. So the Fan Man actually may have changed heavyweight history.

Larry Merchant: Who could forget the sideshow, amazing, phenomenal, bizarre situation known as Fan Man. HBO unbelievably had shots of him gliding around the ring. I would suppose they did not alert us because who could have known what was going to happen and what was on this guy's mind? I am not even sure if we knew we had the footage until after the event. My recollection is we did have it afterwards and we were able to show this guy flying around the stadium like Batman. He was circling around the arena. Who could have imagined that he wanted to swoop in on the ring itself?

Chuck Giampa: One thing I remember about doing that fight was, as a judge, you get used to the sounds of a fight. The sounds of the crowd, or even the sounds of the TV commentators who are quite close to the judge's table. There are certain sounds that you hear. Fan Man actually came right over me. The crowd began to make the strangest sound. I remember hearing a motor coming down over me, and I could not take my eyes off of the ring because of the continuing action. Time had not been called yet. It was the strangest sound I could have ever imagined hearing at a boxing match. I saw this man fly into the ring and saw two rigs bending over the top rope. What had happened was his parachute had gotten stuck on the lights, and he was hanging there. I was actually sitting in the part of the arena where Riddick Bowe's family was sitting, His wife was pregnant at the time, and his entourage surrounded her. This was back when cell phones were the big brick-looking types. I remember Bowe's camp rushing over to Fan Man and just beating him up; he got beat up. They literally carried him out of the ring and onto the floor where they continued to beat him up. The other thing I remember is the actions of Jesse Jackson. He was everywhere. Quite often the commission would put the judges' stools on a little platform that was above the actual floor of the arena. Jackson almost knocked me off my stool. Mills Lane then called time out when Fan Man came in. We did not know what was going on; we didn't know if another glider was going to come in. We were not sure anything, so everyone was pretty uptight at first. I am standing on the platform, with my back to the ring, looking in the direction that Fan Man had swooped in on. I remember Jesse Jackson jumping up on the platform in front of me, his back was to my chest. There was pure chaos going on at this point, but I remember pushing him off of the platform. I asked him, "What are you doing?" He told me, "I am not going back down there." I told him, "I don't care what you do, but you're not coming back here." Jerry Roth was sitting across from me, and he actually saw at the last minute when Fan Man swooped in. He saw the whole thing;

one could not help but see it, it was a strange sight. I had no idea what it was initially, just such a different sound, a whirring of a motor. A lot of people ask me in interviews what my most memorable fight was. I always tell them, the Fan Man fight.

Jerry Roth: I don't remember specific details of what exactly happened, I just remember that when Fan Man did land, he was beaten to a pulp. I remember a lot of cell phones bouncing off his head. It was amazing to watch the thing happen from start to finish.

Kathy Duva: Pure chaos. I was sitting next to my late husband Dan at the time of the delay. Dan used to get really engaged when it came to watching fights and did not like to be bothered while he was taking a fight in. I saw this man flying towards the ring from the direction of the nosebleeds. I could not believe what I was seeing. I nudged Dan a couple times trying to get his attention, but he just told me to shut up so he could watch the fight. Before he could tell me to shut up a second time, Fan Man landed. It was scary. He actually got caught on the lights that are above the ring. Bowe's security people beat him up pretty badly. I remember Jesse Jackson knocking Bowe's pregnant wife over as he was trying to get away from Fan Man. He must have thought it was an attempt on his life. Dan was pissed off at the time because Holyfield was beating up Bowe to the point where a knockout could have been possible. Dan viewed the delay as a stroke of luck for Bowe. We put blankets on Evander and waited for the situation to calm down a little bit. We must have been sitting there waiting for twenty minutes or so. It was a bizarre to say the least.

Jim Lampley: Someone had been tracking him relatively early. I had a note from the truck that something was going on above Caesars Palace. I looked up a couple minutes later; all of a sudden, this man descends upon Vegas. He landed eight feet away from us. I knew it was a possibility, but it still came out of the blue. It was one thing to think he would actually land. I have a vague memory that Bowe was starting to rally, and then Fan Man's visit may have interrupted him.

Evander Holyfield: Fan Man didn't mean that much to me. When he landed, I wanted to make sure that I got out of the way of the lights. A couple years before, a fighter had died when the lights fell on him. I wanted to make sure that did not happen to me. Once they took him off the ring, I didn't know what to do next. There was a lot of confusion as to what the next step was. I was upset because Fan Man had let Riddick off the hook. I was fighting a masterpiece fight before that guy crashed the party. That fight would not have made it to the tenth round if Fan Man had never landed. That guy gave Riddick a break.

Riddick Bowe: At the time I could not help but think that the whole thing was a sham. I felt like it was a hoax or something. It seemed planned. I was cool until I heard about my wife being taken to the hospital. I was told that she had fainted but later found out that dumbass Jesse Jackson had knocked her over. She was pregnant at the time and that had me concerned. Rock told me she was not in a life-threatening situation, so I agreed to resume the fight. I was worried about her though, and I think it affected me in the second half of the fight.

Shelly Finkel: The Fan Man I thought helped Evander because I thought Riddick was getting tired and the time got him some rest.

Lou Dibella: I was sitting behind Rock Newman, and Fan Man's feet literally flew just a couple of feet from my head on his way to the ring. It was wild seeing these feet dangling in my face out of nowhere. If it had taken place post-9/11, who knows what the vibe would have. I have to imagine the situation could have been crazier than it was.

Harold Lederman: The first thing I could see when he landed was Rock Newman grabbing him and hurtling him into a mob. It was an amazing thing to watch. That guy got his butt kicked like you would not believe. It was a very confusing sequence of events.

Joe Cortez: Fan Man—I was at home watching on TV. I have learned to expect the unexpected in boxing but that *really* was the unexpected. That to me is the craziest thing I have ever heard of in my sport at any time ever.

Fan Man, by definition, attacked Caesars Palace that night. He didn't have a bomb, he didn't kill anyone, but he terrorized thousands of people emotionally for ten minutes or so. It takes quite a pair of balls to swoop into a live sporting event unannounced. If there had been snipers on the roof, he could have been shot. To compound the danger in such a feat, he was also was using a motor. A very big motor that could have brought the entire light setup down, potentially killing a lot of people. In having a motor that he could control manually, it was impossible to argue that he just happened to land in the biggest event for one thousand miles either way. He planned the jump and then navigated himself to the stadium. He was reckless and caused a desperate situation. You won't find many people that have too much sympathy for the beating laid down on him upon his arrival. His act was the ultimate definition of criminal mischief.

There was confusion abound during the twenty-three-minute delay. Commissioner Marc Ratner had a solid disaster on his hands. HBO and their TVKO broadcast had been disrupted; men were toting guns and shouting. The crowd was uneasy and tense. Given the perceived danger that everyone in the stadium felt, it was conceivable that both men could refuse to continue. The oddity of the situation gave both men the right to walk away and try again down the road. Bowe, who was benefiting from the delay, was informed that his wife Judy Bowe had passed out at ringside and was being transported to the hospital. To complicate matters, she was in her second trimester; the baby was due relatively soon. As a man, if your wife and your unborn child are hospitalized, anyone could understand if you walked away. Given the fact that Holyfield was getting the better of the fight to that point, Bowe had even more reason to duck out of the fight. Unlike Kermit Cintron, Riddick Bowe did not use the excuses available to him to roll out. He would agree to continue to fight despite the gigantic distractions that were tugging at him mentally.

Fan Man's flight would reach beyond Caesars Palace; he actually may have had a legit effect on the history books.

**Chuck Giampa:** **The interesting thing about that fight, as I remember, is that all of the judges agreed on every single round except for the round with the Fan Man. One of us had it 10–9 for Bowe, the other had it 10–9 for Holyfield, the other judge had it even. I ended up scoring the fight 114–114, six rounds to six rounds; the other two had it seven rounds to five for Holyfield. As judges, we learned that you never know the length of a referee's time out, that particular disruption was twenty-one minutes long, therefore it was hard to remember what happened before the interruption. What I learned from that fight is no matter what the time out is for, be it a mouth piece or a loose piece of tape, always write down your score because there is no telling how long the delay is going to last for. This is a point that I have stressed at seminars; it is because of that specific round. Here is a fight that was so close, so nip and tuck, the seventh round made all the difference. I use that round at every seminar I teach. It's a great learning tool for would-be judges. That round changed history for the better or worse, depending on if you're for Evander or Riddick.**

The seventh round decided the fight. Evander was winning the fight on the surface; according to the actual scorecards, he was only slightly ahead. That one questionable round decided everything. Fan Man (RIP) can rest knowing his act, his feat, possibly changed boxing history. It was a colossal event in the ring and outside of it. The ramifications of the aerial intrusion go way beyond Jesse Jackson's "bullet dodging" or Marc Ratner's administrative disaster. It changed the boxing history books, and at the end of the day, that is the biggest injustice. It affected the scoring; it affected the rhythm of the fight. Evander Holyfield was in a marvelous groove at the time of the delay, and who knows what would have happened if he had been allowed to continue upon his destructive course.

As the seventh round resumed, one fact became readily apparent. Riddick Bowe was the lesser man on this night. Evander was moving and bouncing, popping his jab, potshotting the slower man. Riddick, clearly not warmed up, was plodding and chasing. Riddick would later tell a writer that "Holyfield boxed his ears off" in the last third of the fight. It was a truly master display of pugilism. Larry Merchant, on the call for HBO, told viewers, "Riddick Bowe appeared to be showing signs of fatigue before the delay." One would think that a twenty-one-minute delay in the middle of the fight would give any well-conditioned athlete ample time to recuperate physically. The problem was Bowe was overweight and undertrained for the fight. He also had to be concerned about his family, his hospitalized wife and unborn child. Adding to Riddick's difficulties was Evander's reformation of strategy. Evander had learned from the first fight and executed Emanuel Steward's game plan to a tee. Evander would ride out a rough moment or two to regain the heavyweight championship of the world. Riddick Bowe, the young upstart, was all of a sudden the former heavyweight champion. Bowe's unfortunate situation was of his own making. An unacceptable training camp and nonsensical personal decisions left Riddick Bowe unprepared to defend the titles he had won. The hunger that had driven him to the top of the sport was gone. The whispers about his lack of commitment to the sport now had new life. The writers and soothsayers that observed the sport were sure to question just how good Riddick Bowe was. Was he a flash in the pan? Riddick knew all of these, and as he headed into the dressing room, he thought to himself "What the fuck do I do now?"

Riddick Bowe had come into camp for the Holyfield fight weighing just under 300 pounds. If one considers the fact that Bowe's optimum weight for combat was 235 pounds, there can be no doubt that Bowe lost the fight in camp, not in the ring. You can't come into camp looking like Dan Rafael and expect to come out looking like Lex Luger. That is not a winning formula at the highest level of the sport. Generally, professional boxers can shed twenty to twenty-five pounds before fights without being too drained to be effective. Fighters have the weight class they compete in, and then they have their walk around weight. For most boxers, an acceptable walk around weight is twenty to thirty pounds above the weight class they compete in. It is vital for fighters to not get carried away with their freedom between engagements. Training camp is a crucible designed for two things: to sharpen your craft and to slim you down. Once a fight is over, a fighter will go back to a normal lifestyle and a less strict diet. Riddick's biggest problem was his failure to adhere to this very basic rule. Riddick had no concept of personal restraint between gigs. Riddick would walk around between fights almost fifty-five to sixty pounds above his competitive weight. That's almost thirty pounds north of training camp weight. Coming into his training camp so heavy put Riddick behind the eight ball. The sheer amount of weight he had to lose was off the charts. It is very stressful on the body to shed fifty or sixty pounds in a two-month window. Compounding the difficulty of such a task was Riddick's tendency to indulge in clandestine junk food sessions. These binges really offset the efforts of team Bowe's attempt to keep Riddick in shape. In the ring, and during the workouts, Riddick was a hard worker. It was his behavior in his own time that undermined the training camps. Riddick loved to eat. He had grown up hungry. With the world at his feet, he wanted to enjoy the most basic of pleasures. It's not a personal flaw to enjoy eating fried food and Snickers bars. It is, however, a professional flaw when you are the heavyweight champion. When you have a planet full of contenders, chomping at the bit to beat your brains in. Riddick knew in his heart, that if he were to regain a heavyweight title belt, it would take a change in attitude before anything. The Holyfield loss was a big step back on the surface. Internally, it was viewed as spilled milk. Time would tell.

**Larry Merchant:** The questions about Bowe centered on his toughness and his grit and his vision to be a serious fighter. He had problems with self-restraint. He had problems with his weight. That more than anything was the main reason there was a question in the air as to whether or not he was as tough as a heavyweight champion had to be. He even mused to me once that he was thinking of building a kitchen in his own bedroom to save him the walk downstairs when he was hungry! That was him; he was sort of a big kid that way. This disposition played into the result of the second fight if you look at the weight differential. He came in heavier than he did in the first fight. He was not in good condition. Bowe was trying to hold on to what he had, as opposed to going for what he wanted. He fought the first fight like a guy going for what he wanted; he fought the second fight, in terms of his conditioning, like a guy trying to defend what he had. I didn't see the same hunger I had in the first fight

# 18
# Comeback Trail

The comeback fight is another clockwork aspect of the sport of boxing. When a star is defeated, the challenge falls upon his handlers to resell their product to the public. A loss in boxing is highly damaging to a fighter's reputation; it can be even more damaging to their finances depending on the fighter. There is, however, a difference between a contender and a champion. If a contender loses, it can set back the arc of a career for years. In some cases, the contender never recovers. In boxing you *can't* lose on the way up. It opens up the possibility of never getting a shot. Champions, on the other hand, have it a little easier after a loss. A champion is a proven world-class performer. Other sanctioning bodies are more inclined to give them a favorable ranking, thus making it easier to climb back into the mix. Provided the defeated champion wins in the wake of a loss. The comeback fight is very important. As Rock Newman went about plotting Riddick's next excursion, he knew it was important for Riddick to win and look good doing it. Adding to Riddick's difficulties were his rankings after the title loss. The sanctioning bodies blessed Riddick with the type of ranking that would make a title shot realistic: three or four fights down the road

**Riddick Bowe:** That pissed me off. I had barely lost my titles and then the sanctioning bodies screwed me over. The WBC didn't even have me in the top ten! It made no sense how I was rated after losing my titles, especially by the WBC.

The ranking of Riddick Bowe in the wake of his defeat was nothing short of a joke. The comings and goings of the good ole boy network were in full effect. Nevertheless, team Bowe had to move forward. Informed scribes and the fans knew that Bowe was a top-flight heavyweight. Paying any attention to the politics of the sport was useless. Rock Newman, god bless him, would begin a losing streak of sorts as it pertained to his matchmaking. A comeback fight should always pit the attraction versus the tomato can. The term "tomato can" in boxing refers to walkover opponent. Much like the fools that Hacksaw Jim Duggan used to beat up on WWF Superstars. Rock Newman picked a tamato can that took some effort to open: the type of tamato can that you have to pat on the bottom to get the contents out. Why Rock would match Riddick Bowe, an offensive fighter, with a notorious defensive fighter in a projected showcase fight is beyond rationale. Sometimes fighters opt for tough comeback fights. Like Roy Jones handpicking Glenn Johnson.

Enter Buster Mathis Jr. Buster Mathis was slightly better than an entry-level heavyweight. Buster Mathis Jr. was the current USBA heavyweight champion. He had defeated Tyrell Biggs by unanimous decision to win the vacated trinket title. Buster would carry some pedigree with him into the ring. Buster was the son of Buster Mathis Sr. Buster Sr. had served as a gatekeeper heavyweight in the sixties. He had even challenged the legendary Muhammad Ali for the heavyweight championship of the world. Buster was not a physical threat to Riddick at that point, but he could damage him from a PR standpoint. While he lacked power, Buster was the proud owner of an extremely difficult style to penetrate. Buster, unlike his father, was slick and elusive. A poor man's Bernard Hopkins is the best description. Like Hopkins, it's hard to look good against Mathis even if you win. Fighting a defensive fighter is always tricky proposition. It's even more difficult to score an impressive victory against such an opponent. On paper, it made perfect sense to pursue Buster as a comeback fight; in the ring, however, it was a shortsighted decision. The whole point of a comeback fight for a defeated champion is to showcase what he does best. Landing clean hard punches is what Bowe does best. Against a slickster like Buster Mathis Jr., that was an uphill battle. The fight would take place on August 13, 1994, at Convention Hall in Atlantic City, New Jersey. Riddick Bowe encountered some difficulty in his comeback fight.

Buster Mathis was not a difficult out for Riddick Bowe. Bowe pushed Mathis around the ring like a rag doll for four rounds, hurting him and bullying him. The result of the fight seemed a foregone conclusion. Toward the end of the fourth round, Riddick Bowe dropped Mathis to his knees with a left hook, without thinking he clocked Buster again while Buster was down. That is a taboo act in the sport of boxing. It usually warrants an immediate disqualification. Roy Jones Jr., one of the greatest fighters of all time, saw his perfect record fly by the wayside because he hit a fighter when the fighter was down on a knee. Bowe clearly had done the same thing, and it appeared that he could suffer another career setback. Such a decision could cripple his boxing career. As Bowe awaited the decision, Larry Hazzard and Gary Shaw of the New Jersey Athletic Control Board huddled in a small circle and essentially held Bowe's career in their hands. It was decided that Riddick Bowe was the winner. HBO replays showed a different story. The replays showed Riddick Bowe violating boxing rules. Riddick Bowe was clearly the better fighter, but so was Roy Jones. Unlike RJJ, Riddick Bowe dodged the landmine and would be enabled to continue his championship quest. After such an outing, conventional wisdom would seem to dictate a more offensive fighter the next time around. This is where matchmaking comes into play. The outcome of the fight did not help Riddick Bowe's stock amongst most respected boxing minds. Riddick Bowe needed a firefight. Unfortunatley, his next opponent would make that next to impossible.

The next foe for Riddick Bowe was highly touted prospect Larry Donald. Larry Donald saw himself as the next Ali, something him and Bowe had in common. Larry possessed a very defensive style, one that forced his opponents to chase him. On the surface, it appeared that Larry was yet another fighter that is difficult to look good against. Larry Donald was an ambitious former Olympian; he boasted a 16–0 record and was looking to make his mark against the highly regarded Bowe. Even though Riddick Bowe was still reeling from the Holyfield loss, many still saw him as the de facto number one man in the division.

**Larry Merchant:** **Certainly I remember many people seeing Riddick Bowe as the preeminent heavyweight in the world after the Holyfield loss. It was not as if Evander had defeated him convingcly, it was a close split-decision loss. The general view was that if Bowe was in shape, he was the best. The problem was he was not at his best in those in-between fights. Riddick Bowe was a well-schooled fighter, but he appeared to drop out of school for a few fights.**

Even though Riddick did not hold the titles, he was still held to a championship standard by the media and fans. He was expected to turn in dynamite performances every time out. Compounding the challenge for Bowe was the type of fighters he was matched with during that period in his career. One would think that the logical thing to do would be to put him in the ring with offensive fighters that prefer to trade. Manny Pacquaio, who many see as the number one fighter in the world today, is matched with offensive fighters that play to his strengths. Bob Arum knows styles, that helps Manny's overall presentation to the boxing public. Riddick Bowe, during a crucial point in his career, was not afforded such a luxury. Matchmaking was not a team Bowe strength.

**Thell Torrence:** **Rock thought he had his hand on the pulse; he had all these key fights out there. Riddick was on top of the world; his selection at that time was in the best interest of Riddick financially, and sometimes we felt it was wrong, but at the end of the day, we could only give our opinion. Rock Newman had the final say.**

Larry Donald, among other things, seemed to have a big mouth in the lead up to the fight. At first it was just seen as playful rhetoric, common to any prizefight. It began to get over the top as the weeks progressed and quietly, covertly, Riddick Bowe's blood was beginning to boil.

**Riddick Bowe:** **All throughout training camp, this man was talking shit. Nonstop. Calling me a chump and a pussy, at first I didn't think much about it, but after six weeks of the bullshit, it started to piss me off. While he was runnin' his mouth, I didn't actually get to see him. That motherfucker didn't say shit at the first press conference announcing the fight. But once he was in his camp and he didn't have to see me, all of a sudden I'm hearing all this bullshit. The Monday of fight week, I saw him for the first time since the first press conference, and I lost it. I didn't lose it right away though. When we did our stare down, he started talking again; he said some shit I don't need to repeat. Without thinking, I gave him a two-piece right there on the spot. I got it in too, ha-ha.**

Give him a two-piece he did. In yet another infamous piece of boxing history, Riddick Bowe punched Larry Donald in the face twice before a national press core in Los Angeles, California. It was on every TV, radio show, and newspaper in the civilized world. To many, however, the seemingly unprovoked actions of Riddick Bowe were not very civilized. People across the nation derided Bowe as a young cocky, dumb kid. His own hometown newspaper, the *New York Daily News*, furnished a back page labeling Riddick a "Brownsville bum." The backlash would continue throughout fight week and into Saturday when the fight took place. HBO opened their broadcast, teeing off on Riddick Bowe and his actions. George Foreman labeled him a villain and called for some type of sanction. One would think that press conference punches would be enough controversy for one fight, but with promotions involving Riddick Bowe, the party never seemed to stop. There was another controversy that erupted when the two camps congregated in Las Vegas.

**Marc Ratner:** In our rule book at that time, you could have a ring size from sixteen to twenty feet. Riddick was a puncher and Larry was a runner. The bigger ring was better suited to Larry's style. Rock Newman requested a small ring (eighteen-foot ring) and pointed out that it was within the rules to do so. His request was historically significant; from that point on we eliminated camps being able to choose the size of the ring and standardized the size of the ring for every fight. Twenty feet.

Larry Donald's camp would be infuriated upon their arrival to Las Vegas when they learned that Rock Newman had laid down an eighteen-foot ring. He also did so before the arrival of Larry's handlers. Many saw this as an immense competitive advantage for Riddick Bowe. Rock Newman was well within the rules, and the decision stood despite a furious protest from Donald's camp.

**Larry Merchant:** I'm telling you what, Larry Donald was way too young and green to be fighting in the major leagues of the division anyway. But after he was socked in his face at a press conference and seemingly forced to fight an awesome puncher in a

> small ring, I still to this day wonder why they went through with the fight. I would have pulled him out. I think I said that on the eventual broadcast. There was a lot of unprofessionalism surrounding that promotion from the Riddick Bowe's camp

The fight itself paled in comparison to the drama that preceded it. Larry Donald was a very game runner. He spent most of the fight running as fast as he could in the face of an offensive juggernaut. Riddick Bowe got a great workout but a dull fight. Larry Donald danced and pranced around the ring but never really seemed interested in fighting. Larry threw less then 10 punches a round. Riddick Bowe coasted to a twelve-round decision. He then collected an easy $1,000,000 purse. Based on the lack of action, the general impression was that Riddick Bowe had not been impressive. Riddick and Larry Donald mended fences after the fight. In a gesture of sportsmanship and goodwill, the two men called a joint press conference a couple of months after the fight. They shook hands; Larry agreed to drop his pending lawsuit against Riddick Bowe. It was a happy ending to an ugly situation. Riddick Bowe needed an opponent that was not going run. He needed a fighter that would showcase his awesome offensive skills. Rock Newman matched Bowe with such a fighter for once, that fighter was WBO heavyweight champion Herbie Hide.

# 19
# And Once Again

Herbie Hide held the WBO heavyweight championship; Herbie would be defending his title for the first time. Born in Nigeria, he had immigrated to the United Kingdom and found his niche in the sport of boxing. Herbie Hide had since progressed through the ranks of the domestic British boxing scene; the champion was ready to make a statement to the world. Herbie Hide was chiseled customer that was held in semi-high esteem by boxing critics. A rough and tough bruiser with intelligence. He had serviceable craft and an iron chin. Seemingly, Herbie Hide was a very live dog headed into the fight. He would also be making his American/HBO debut. To many, the fight represented Bowe's first trip back to competitive boxing since the Holyfield loss. Riddick Bowe's stock had dropped slightly because of his less-than-scintillating performance against Larry Donald. Bowe's purse was an indicator of the drop off. He would make less than a million ($500,000) for the first time in two years. The fight turned out to be just as action-packed as any of the fights Riddick Bowe took part in beforehand. Herbie Hide, unlike Riddick's two comeback foes, had zero trepidation about getting into an all-out war with Riddick Bowe. The first two rounds were dominated by Herbie Hide's hand speed and thudding punches. He was moving from side to side. He also was moving toward Riddick's left, which is a textbook way to neutralize a right-handed power puncher. Herbie Hide also intentionally head butted Bowe while they were clinched at close quarters. In the second round, Herbie attempted to head butt Riddick several times before he actually connected. It was so overt and blatant that Richard Steele threatened to disqualify Herbie Hide if it happened again. That's a significant threat, considering he had not any points deducted thus far in the fight. Herbie Hide continued his unexpected assault in round three, badly staggering Riddick Bowe with a barrage of punches, bringing the sparse MGM Grand crowd to its feet. The fight suddenly changed directions in a very strange fashion. In the middle of an exchange, Herbie Hide was knocked down to the canvas seemingly on his own. Richard

Steele ruled it a slip. A dazed Herbie Hide rose to his feet, unbalanced and glassy eyed. No one knew what to make of it; no one saw the punch that caused so much damage. Riddick Bowe would pounce on Herbie, redepositing him on the canvas fifteen seconds later. No one seemed to know what to make of Herbie Hide's sudden dire situation. It was confusing to everyone.

**Riddick Bowe:** I didn't know if he was playing possum or what. He had me going just fifteen seconds before he was "hurt." It was strange, I thought he was tired and that was causing all the knockdowns. I know for a fact that the punch at the end of the round hurt him; there was nothing confusing about that.

Riddick Bowe landed a ferocious uppercut on Hide's chin, sending him down for the fourth time in the round, the third time officially. The bell saved Hide, but there were those ringside that thought the fight should have been over. Richard Steele called the first knockdown a slip, saving Herbie from a technical knockout. In the State of Nevada, there is a three knockdown rule. The rule states if a fighter is knocked down three times, that constitutes a technical knockout. HBO replays, however, showed no actual punch landing. Those that were critical of Richard Steele can go ahead and prove that the knockdown was the result of the punch.

The savage exchanges would continue throughout the fight. Both men would taste each other's power several times. Herbie Hide, however, touched the canvas nine times en route to being stopped in the sixth round. The strange aspect about all of the knockdowns is that Riddick only appeared to land three or four clean punches over the course of the fight. It appeared too many; Herbie was going down because of sheer exhaustion. Yet again, Riddick Bowe had won, but the manner in which he did left just a little bit to be desired. Not everyone felt that Herbie Hide was a pushover.

**Harold Lederman:** I consider the Herbie Hide fight to be one of Riddick Bowe's most impressive victories. Hide was strong, talented, and courageous. He had Bowe hurt a couple times. Hide had a real shot at winning. Bowe slowly wore him down and pulled it out. Riddick does not get enough credit for that fight. Herbie Hide was a tough, hard-nosed fighter.

**Richard Steele:** Herbie tried all types of tricks. All types of head fakes and feints. None of it worked. He simply had nothing for Riddick at that point. Riddick was a hell of a fighter. Power, speed, and he had Eddie Futch. Riddick was way too much for Herbie Hide; it was kind of a mismatch.

Riddick had been wobbled by some of Hide's punches; to some, he seemed slightly overweight. The victory would be further cheapened by HBO, who refused to recognize the tilt as a title bout to its viewing audience.

Ironically, the WBO title is very credible nowdays. In fact, Manny Pacquaio's record-setting seventh world title was a WBO belt. So while at the time the belt was not held in high esteem, Riddick Bowe has the right to call himself a two-time heavyweight champion. During the postfight interview, Riddick Bowe and Larry Merchant bantered over whom Riddick Bowe should fight next. Larry rightfully questioned the resume of Riddick's past few opponents. When asked whom he would like to fight next, Riddick mentioned Jorge Luis Gonzalez. Riddick Bowe met a lot of fighters over the course of his career that had gotten under his skin, but Jorge Luis Gonzalez took trash talk and personal attacks to another level. Another stratosphere.

# 20
# A Lion vs. a Hyena

**Harold Lederman:** Jorge Gonzalez was an MGM fighter. He was their guy. He was a big draw there, and the hotel really supported him. They wanted him to defeat Bowe so they could stage a title fight at the casino. The rivalry between the two got ugly, real ugly.

Riddick Bowe and Jorge Luis Gonzalez had a history. Jorge had defeated Riddick in the amateurs. He did not let Riddick forget that fact. He was loud, brash, and a contender. Much like David Haye today. And like David Haye, Luis would prove to be more sound then fury. It is not a mystery why Riddick had so much angst and disgust for Jorge Luis Gonzalez.

**Riddick Bowe:** I wanted to knock that motherfucker out. It didn't matter if it was in the ring or not. Some of the things he said just didn't make any sense. He told me he was going to beat up my wife, eat my children; he told me he was a lion and I was a hyena and he was going to eat my heart.

In an event, that was shades of the Larry Donald press conference. Riddick Bowe came within a whisker of fighting yet another opponent during fight week. This encounter took place in the dining room of the MGM Grand in front of cameras and beat reporters. With ice and food trays flying, the two jawed at each other and had to be separated. This had become a staple of the marketing campaign. The two fighters staged press conferences that bordered upon offensive to anyone who could hear them. Things got so out of control the week of the fight, that the Nevada State athletic commission ruled that the two fighter's could not appear at press conferences together. They would have to do it separately.

They also would not be allowed to weigh in at the same time. The rivalry would continue to simmer on fight night when famed referee Mills Lane visited both fighters for prefight instructions.

**Terry Lane:** **The second fight my father took me too was the Riddick Bowe-Gonzalez fight at the MGM Grand. My little brother and me happened to go into the locker room with our dad before the fight. We visited with both camps. We go into Riddick's dressing room, and as always, he was the consummate gentleman. My dad always made a point of asking the fighters to shake hands after the fight if there was some acrimony in the air during the promotion. He is old-fashioned and always did things that way. He would do it to avoid any problems or skirmishes after the fight. My dad and I went in to see Riddick first. Dad gives him the instructions; my dad asks him if after the fight, no matter the result, would Riddick would shake Jorge's hand. Riddick said yes, and his corner said yes. We then went into Gonzales's dressing room and went through the same routine. When Dad asked him about the idea of shaking Riddick's hand no matter the result, they said no. Gonzales then began speaking Spanish. I was told later that he said something to the effect, "In the jungle, you have lions and hyenas. I am a lion, he is a hyena." So after that my dad had to go back to Bowe's dressing room and inform him that the handshake would not be happening.**

Riddick Bowe vs. Jorge Luis Gonzalez took place on June 17, 1995. Riddick Bowe's purse returned to seven-figure range at a clean $1,000,000. Jorge's bark would prove to be much worse than his bite. George Foreman told HBO viewers in reference to Gonzalez, "Where there is smoke, there is usually more smoke." George's words proved to be prophetic; Jorge provided zero resistance to an emotional Riddick Bowe.

**Riddick Bowe:** **I am not going to say I wanted to kill him because that's not true. But based on everything that was go-**

> ing on before the fight, I wanted to knock him out, I wanted to punish him. Talking about eating my heart, talked about my wife, my children. I wanted to hurt him more than anyone I fought in my entire career. Mills Lane saved his punk ass in the sixth round; I might have really hurt him if he didn't call the fight.

Riddick Bowe battered Gonzalez from pillar to post en route to a sixth-round TKO. It was Riddick's most awesome performance since his initial conquest of Evander Holyfield. Many touted Riddick as the number one heavyweight in the world in the wake of the victory. Riddick appeared to be in perfect working condition. Riddick Bowe showed some of the tools that had been hibernating for the last couple of fights. He bullied Gonzalez around the ring, landing power punch after power punch. Gonzalez was one of those fighters who fought in the amateurs for much too long. He was exposed in the fight as just that, a very good amateur. Riddick was on a three-fight winning streak headed into the fight. This was the first time he seemed to be in championship form during the streak. Many on the boxing scene were skeptical of Riddick Bowe. They doubted his motivation to get in tip-top shape. The Gonzalez fight was a resounding answer to those questions. Riddick Bowe was back and ready for a meaningful fight. The heavyweight scene was in shambles. Michael Moore had taken the titles from Evander Holyfield, only to be knocked out by George Foreman. George Forman, determined to not defend his titles against anyone that he perceived as a threat, was refusing to take on top-flight contenders. George Foreman held the titles for almost a year before defending them; he was stripped of one of the belts in the process. While a fight between Foreman and Bowe would have been big business at the box office, George Foreman, in the twilight of his career, was not going to assume the type of risk that accompanied a championship fight with Riddick Bowe. A much-talked-about fight with Mike Tyson flew by the boards. Although Tyson was no longer a guest of the government, he had no intention of going straight to a fight with Riddick Bowe upon his release from jail. Tyson knew he could make big-time money fighting a stiff, and fight stiffs he did. He could have made even more money fighting Bowe but did not want to risk getting knocked out.

# Act Three

Riddick Bowe had no notable opponents to pursue. There was only one logical path to solidify his return to the top of the division. A third fight with Evander Holyfield. A rubber match was not Riddick's first choice, but it made fiscal sense and would cement the two men in history. Riddick Bowe wanted a third crack at Evander Holyfield.

**Riddick Bowe:** **I wanted that fight for several reasons. I wanted to avenge the only loss of my career. He had gotten a little lucky in that second fight; his game plan had thrown me off a little bit, and with Fan Man, I never really got in a good rhythm. I also knew if I got past Evander, I would be in line for a title shot. I didn't have any bad feelings against Evander, but I did want to beat him convincingly.**

The third fight contained a story line that dominated everyone's thinking in the lead-up. After Evander's heavyweight championship, April 22, 1994, defeat at the hands of Michael Moore, Evander was admitted to the hospital complaining of shoulder pain. It quickly became clear to doctors that Evander was having complications with his heart. After a battery of tests, it was determined that Evander had two problems with his heart. He was diagnosed with a stiff heart. A condition that handicaps the heart's ability to spread oxygen to the muscles and tissues. Evander was also diagnosed with an atria septal, a tiny hole in the heart. These revelations led most boxing fans and writers to plead with Holyfield to retire. In agreeing to fight Riddick Bowe, he was seemingly putting his life at risk. Evander ignored everyone's personal appeals and continued his fight career after being "healed" by an evangelist. Of course he paid the man a couple grand for the procedure, but according to Evander, he was as good as new. The Mayo Clinic and other independent doctors supported Evander's claims. Even though various parties and the Nevada

State Athletic Commission cleared Evander Holyfield, there were some reservations in boxing circles about whether or not it was ethical to let him fight.

Commission doctors had also been speculating about the origin of Evander Holyfield's heart abnormalities. Some of those in the medical sector of the commission noticed that Evander's problems were consistent with HGH use. During the medical hearing before the third Bowe fight, the commission questioned Evander Holyfield about HGH use. Evander denied the allegations; since there was no test to combat HGH, the allegations remained just that. Many years later, Evander Holyfield was connected to a steroid bust headed by the Drug Enforcement Administration. An antiaging clinic, in Jupiter, Florida, was the target of the investigation. Federal agents connected Holyfield to the drug ring through an alias found on the client delivery list. According to records recovered in the sting, "Evan Fields" picked up three vials of testosterone, two vials of Glucor, and "related injection supplies." Five weeks later, according to the records, Evan Fields returned and purchased five vials of Saizen. Evan Fields also purchased a "form" of human growth hormone during the visit. Evan Field's profile contained Evander Holyfield's phone number. *Sports Illustrated* called the phone number located in Evan Field's profile and got Evander on the phone personally. Evan Field's address was eerily similar to Evander's: 794, Evander, Fairfield, Georgia. Evan Fields and Evander Holyfield also shared the same birthday, October 19, 1962. In an era of Roger Clemens and Marion Jones, one has to wonder why the national media did not press Evander on his connection to "Evan Fields."

**Evander Holyfield: Never used HGII or steroids. I could not tell you why I had those heart complications, but by the grace of God, I was able to see those problems through and continue to fight.**

Riddick Bowe: I never believed that Evander was on the juice. I have heard that from different people, but I know Evander personally, and I doubt that he would do something to put my life in danger. It didn't matter if he was on something or not. He was going to get it in that third fight. I owed him one.

> **Dr Martha Goodman:** I became a ring physician in 1994, although I worked as a neurological consultant to the commission the year before that. In the latter capacity, I was asked to examine Meldrick Taylor and George Foreman and Evander Holyfield. I was a ring physician from 1994-2005, and Chief Ringside Physician 2004-2005. I was Chairman of the NSAC's Medical Advisory Board---a governor appointed position from 2001-2007. Currently, I consider myself a boxing safety advocate and have written a monthly column for The Ring magazine since 2004. I have worked perhaps more than 500 fight cards, and have a private practice in Neurology in Las Vegas, NV since 1988. It has never been proven that Evander ever used PED's. However, the changes reflected in Evander's heart--detected after his bout against Michael Moorer, could have been from PED use--such as from HGH

The concern for Evander's health was not just limited to the press core or the fans. The third man in the ring that night, Joe Cortez, was aware of Evander's problems.

**Joe Cortez:** I had read that Holyfield had a hole in his heart. I had also read that he went to some voodoo doctor or something and now was cured. Evander was telling people he was brand new again or something. The commission informed me that he had passed all the test and that he was going to be given the green light to fight. His health was in the back of my mind, but I trusted the decision of the commission. They would not put someone's life in danger.

The third fight took place almost three years to the day after the first fight. There would be no title at stake; the championship of each other sufficed. On November 4, 1995, the world saw one of the greatest trilogies in boxing history come to a close. Riddick would make a career high purse of $8,000,000 dollars. Riddick Bowe was primed and ready for the rubber match.

**Riddick Bowe:** This was my chance to right the wrong. I had a good camp and was at a good weight. The doctors had cleared Evander, so I was past the point of being concerned about his safety. I was going in there to knock him out.

The "Final Chapter" was the name of the third promotion. Like the second fight, it took place at Caesars Palace in Las Vegas, Nevada. This was not going to be a heavyweight championship fight. At least not on paper. The court of public of opinion, however, would give the fight a championship feel. Since George Foreman was disintegrating into a paper champion, most boxing writers considered the winner of this fight to be the number one heavyweight in the world. The two men were fighting for perceived heavyweight supremacy. It was also an opportunity to settle the score.

The third fight, in a strange way, was a combination of the first two fights condensed into eight rounds. The first third of the fight resembled the second fight. Evander was dancing, popping his jab, and landing meaningful right hands. Riddick Bowe was upset by the constant movement and continued to stalk Evander, not doing an effective job of cutting off the ring. Evander was a surgeon in the opening round, dominatating the action. In the second round, Evander Holyfield did a 360 tactically. Evander inexplicably put his head on Riddick Bowe's chest and began to trade at close quarters. This twist in the plot transitioned the fight from a sample size of the second fight to a reincarnation of the first fight. Both men were landing big-time shots, getting as good as they got. Many ringside observers were wondering why Evander would abandon his game plan and run the risk of being knocked out. Skeptics, however, assumed that Evander's change in strategy had nothing to do with pride. It must have something to do with his heart. Evander appeared worn; he appeared to lack energy. He was breathing as heavy as anyone had ever seen. As the fight entered the middle rounds, there seemed to be genuine concern that Evander was in a life-threatening situation. Riddick Bowe was one of those that did not seem concerned. He was battering Evander, taking advantage of Holyfield's perceived weakness. People shouted at the ring for the fight to be stopped. Evander looked so bad at certain points that some thought they were watching a death in the ring.

**Evander Holyfield:** My heart was fine. I appreciate everyone's concern for my personal safety, but the commission doctors and independent experts had cleared me to fight. Something was wrong with me that night. I had contracted hepatitis A. I had eaten some bad seafood, and I was hit. It sapped me of my energy completely. My eyes were yellow, I was light-headed, but I was not going to let this big rascal get the best of me without a fight.

Evander Holyfield, on the brink of destruction, got off his stool in the sixth round, seemingly headed for an execution. Riddick Bowe, confident his man was a spent force, went after Evander, forsaking some of his tactical advantages. Out of nowhere, Evander landed a jarring left hook that buckled Riddick Bowe's legs and put him in la-la land.

**Riddick Bowe:** Everyone remembers the left hook that he knocked me down with. It hurt, but it was that first left hook that really hurt me. I didn't even feel the second left hook. I was hurt. That is as hurt as I have ever been in my career. He could've stopped me if he had been able to sustain the punishment. He couldn't. He had nothing left.

**Joe Cortez:** It was yet another great fight, both men went down and both men fought with so much heart and spirit. When Evander took Bowe down, for some reason or another, Holyfield stopped throwing punches. Evander was throwing punches, but there was no power behind them, he had no breath, he had nothing. Evander was literally out on his feet when he had Bowe in trouble; he let Riddick off the hook.

The sixth round was a drama in three acts. The first act was the knockdown, which shocked everyone in attendance. The second act was Riddick Bowe in trouble but Evander not really being able to capitalize. The third act of the round featured rallies by Riddick Bowe. After being close to being knocked out, Riddick Bowe recovered and was controlling the action as the round came to a close. The round was very much like the tenth round of the first fight. Riddick Bowe, to this day, does not get the credit that Holyfield received after a similar act of courage.

Evander slumped into his corner stool and looked across the ring. He caught Riddick Bowe looking back at him.

**Riddick Bowe:** **He looked across the ring at me and gave me a little wink. Like, "I got you!" I was already a little pissed about being knocked down and hurt like that by a smaller man. When he started gloating a little bit, I knew it was time to get him out of there.**

Even though Evander appeared to be in trouble, he still displayed just how ornery he could be in the heat of a battle. The seventh round saw both men fight to a stalemate. Riddick Bowe had the upper hand, but he was not dominating like he had been in the earlier rounds. The action picked back up in the eighth round. Evander attacked Riddick to start the round with wide winging shots, attempting to duplicate the success he had enjoyed in the sixth round. It was not to be; while throwing one of those hooks, Evander was caught by a picture-perfect short right hand on the chin. Evander fell flat on his face and struggled to get to his feet. He beat the count but looked like a defeated man as Joe Cortez held his gloves. Joe Cortez asked him if he wanted to continue. Evander opted to continue. Riddick made him pay for it, knocking him into the ropes with a clubbing right hand that prompted commission members, as well as Joe Cortez, to stop the fight. Riddick Bowe had become the first man to knock out Evander Holyfield. He had avenged the lone loss on his record and established himself as the superior boxer between the two. Evander Holyfield was, again, not disgraced in defeat. It seemed at the time that his body was turning on him at age thirty-four; perhaps it was time to call it a day. Perceptions, however, were not reality. Evander was simply suffering from a temporary case of hepatitis A and was in no condition to fight on that particular night. Evander went on to prove that he had plenty left in the tank. His career actually took off in the wake of the loss.

**Jeffery Shultz:** **Holyfield was awful in the third fight. The fact that he was dreadful in that fight and then shaky in the following bout against Bobby Czyz is what led**

many to be concerned about him fighting Mike Tyson. I really never believed Tyson was some indestructible being when he got out of jail, but considering Evander seemed to have nothing left against Bowe, that is what led me to think he had little chance against Tyson. Holyfield even admitted he was awful in Bowe III, saying he had thoughts like "I really want to get out of here"—as in retire. But he later claimed that he had a virus that sapped him of energy during training and the fight. I thought the best quote following the fight came from George Foreman, who said of Holyfield, "He's not going to retire, he's going to expire."

Chuck Giampa: I remember Holyfield knocking down Bowe and trying to finish him off. Evander literally had nothing on his punches. I was amazed Evander could not finish him. Riddick Bowe was *really* hurt after the knockdown. I remember Evander simply running out of gas. I thought after that fight that Evander Holyfield had fought his best fights. I thought he was done as a top-level fighter.

Riddick Bowe, even though he did not hold a title, was now considered the best heavyweight out there. He had rebounded from his only loss to run off four straight victories, including a win over the only man to defeat him. Riddick also had taken part in one of the greatest trilogies in boxing history.

Larry Merchant: I think it is the most underestimated trilogy in recent times. I think in terms of drama, each fight had tremendous drama. The first fight speaks for itself. The second fight contained the Fan Man incident and Holyfield's extraordinary effort. In the third fight, Holyfield, coming back from what appeared to be the dead, knocked Bowe down. It was tremendous drama and a tremendous trilogy; the only others that compare in boxing history were Ali-Frazier, Ali-Norton, and Patterson-Johansson, which by the way was a tremendously dramatic three fights.

Lou Dibella: One of the greatest trilogies in boxing history. No question about it.

Lem Satterfield: The Bowe-Holyfield trilogy, to me, that was the last great one between heavyweights who were in shape. At least, Bowe was in shape for the first and the third. Lots of action, lots of give-and-takes, and the Fan Man, also in the second fight that was won by Holyfield. Historically, it's nowhere near as meaningful as Ali-Frazier, nor has it stood the test of time in memory as far as I am concerned.

Shelly Finkel: A historic trilogy. They are both great guys who gave it their all.

Thom Loverro: **It is the last great stand of the heavyweight division. Little did we know that we were watching the end of heavyweight boxing. It was a great rivalry.**

Many believed that Riddick Bowe would now get the fight that he always wanted. A fight that much of boxing world had been coveting. A date with his schoolmate, Iron Mike Tyson.

# 22

# Tyson

Mike Tyson and Riddick Bowe go back much farther than many people realize. They both grew up in the same section of Brooklyn; they attended the same elementary school and would often see each other during their daily activities. Moving forward, there is a big question in the boxing history: why didn't Riddick Bowe and Mike Tyson ever get in the ring? There are many factors that contributed to this occurrence. Bad timing stands as the biggest reason the fight did not come off. As Bowe was making his push into the upper echelon of the division, Mike Tyson was sent to Indiana State Prison to atone for his alleged sexual misgivings. The time that Tyson was in prison, Bowe was at his apex. It's hard to believe that if Tyson had been acquitted of rape charges, he would have been able to avoid a clash with Bowe. The public would have demanded the fight. It must be pointed out that even if both fighters have been available, it still would have been tricky to make the fight due to a five-hundred-pound entity in the room: HBO.

Mike Tyson and Don King had been loudly unhappy with HBO towards the end of Tyson's contract with the network. Don King wanted two things that HBO was not willing to do. He wanted a lion's share of the PPV profits; he also wanted the network to fire Larry Merchant. Larry Merchant is a cornerstone of HBO boxing; no way in the world the network was going to exchange that for anything. When HBO refused appeasement, Tyson left the network shortly thereafter. The dynamic duo made clear their intentions: at expiration of the contract, they would be leaving the network and going with Showtime. Showtime is HBO's chief rival in boxing television. Tyson leaving HBO was a seismic event at the time. Much bigger than Bob Arum's CBS coup earlier this year. This is why Tyson would go on to be a Showtime fighter for the rest of his career. Riddick Bowe was an HBO fighter. For a fight to have been made, the two networks would need to work together. They proved it was possible when Mike Tyson and Lennox Lewis would meet later in the decade. Even though it was possible, it was not probable. HBO most likely was not too thrilled about losing a cash cow like Tyson to their chief rival in the industry. Internally, HBO could not have been too impressed with Don King and Mike Tyson slandering them in public nonstop.

It would have been an awesome event. Given that they had known each other personally since sixth grade and were two former heavyweight champions; the story lines would have been endless. Stylistically, opinions vary on what exactly would have taken place.

**Lem Satterfield:** Hard to say. We never had a chance to measure Tyson's heart when his team was at its best. Tyson, at his best, never faced a fighter the caliber of Riddick Bowe or Evander Holyfield for that matter. Other than the historical accomplishment of vanquishing Trevor Berbick at the age of twenty, his most defining fights, unfortunately, were his losses.

**Zaira Nazario:** When thinking about boxing styles complementing each other in the creation of a dream match, like the pieces of a perfectly designed puzzle to banquet the public, one cannot avoid to entertain the idea of Riddick "Big Daddy" Bowe vs. Iron Mike Tyson. In Mike Tyson, we had the unusual package of fast-hand speed, power, excellent head and upper body movement. In Riddick Bowe we had athleticism, cleverness in the ring, mastery of the inside game, excellent long- and midrange fighting, powerful combinations of punches, which include a nice compact right uppercut, all while displacing relaxedly in his boxing stage. It would have been a wonderful fight.

**Terry Lane:** My dad was a boxer; he analyzed all the boxers that he spent time with or around. His main criticism of Bowe was he did not seem disciplined. The fight that he always wanted to see was the Bowe-Tyson fight. It would have been a huge fight. Both guys are from Brownsville. Tyson was nowhere near as big as Riddick Bowe. My dad thought that Riddick Bowe would win the fight because of his size, power, and talent.

Bowe's size and hand speed would have been a huge problem for Tyson. Tyson, over his career, had a lot of trouble with big men that could put punches together. Tyson had even more trouble fighting moving backwards. He would have been backed up all night by Bowe's size and activity. Bowe also knew Tyson personally. Any element of fear that Mike usually enjoyed would have been nullified. Tyson would not enjoy any of his usual advantages in the event that a fight with Bowe ever came off.

**Riddick Bowe:** He always respected me. From sixth grade on, Mike Tyson has always given me my respect. I won't say he feared me, but he knew what was up. I certainly never feared him like some of the other clowns that go in the ring with him. If I had ever been able to get him in that ring, I would have tapped that ass. I love him though. I consider him a good friend to this day.

A major problem was everything that was going on with Riddick Bowe and the WBC. Riddick Bowe had said publicly several times that he wanted nothing to do with Don King. Even if that meant boycotting the WBC altogether. To make a fight with Mike Tyson, Bowe's camp would have to deal with Don King directly. Rock Newman and Don King are not exactly justices of the peace. Rock Newman had supplanted Don King as the heavyweight division's premier power broker. Don King was not crazy about this fact; there can be no doubt that particular insecurity influenced the negotiations. Rock Newman and Don King's egos were too big for one single promotion. There is no way one was going to bow to the other.

**Thom Loverro:** I have no particular knowledge of what happened behind the scenes. I suspect the last thing Tyson wanted to do when he came of prison—and Don King—was to put his comeback at risk by fighting Bowe, at least what they thought Bowe was at the time.

Mike Tyson and Don King were passing on the fight. The two of them realized after the Mcneely fight, that they could make a fortune fighting cupcakes. Don King realized after Mike got out of prison that everyone just wanted to see Mike Tyson fight; the public could not care less about whom he was fighting. Boxing insiders and the hardcore fan base wanted to see the Riddick and Tyson, but much like Bob Arum today, Don King did not use his political power to make fans happy. Since Rock Newman was turned down several times by the Tyson camp, he searched for an opponent that would not hurt Bowe's credibility but would not pose too much of a danger at the same time. After a hasty look around the boxing scene, Rock Newman selected the most dangerous man he could have possibly found in the sport. Bad matchmaking had become Rock Newman's staple, but this decision took his matchmaking resume to an all-new low. The boneheaded selection of Andrew Golota, as Riddick Bowe's next opponent, set off a chain of events that no one could have ever predicted.

# Andrew

Andrew Golata had followed the script of so many that had come before him in the sport. He had grown up amid poverty; in becoming a top-level prizefighter, Andrew had delivered himself and his family from a life of hunger and hard knocks. Andrews's opera had begun within the concrete jungles of Warsaw, Poland. The ghetto, as some would call it. Andrew immigrated to America to escape criminal prosecution. Sources in Poland claim it was a fight in a bar that escalated into a gunfight. Make no bones about it. Andrew was from the hood. He would take that rugged disposition into the ring, and it helped his secondary boxing career take off.

Rock Newman saw Golota's record (30–0), saw that it contained no world-class names, and figured it would be the perfect tune up for a potential Tyson fight. Andrew had navigated his way through the gatekeepers of the division but had not really defined himself against a named heavyweight. Rock Newman must not have been watching much film. They also were not exactly on their Ps and Qs when it came to keeping Bowe in shape. Mackie Shilstone did his part, but he was only one man. Eddie Futch and Thell Torrence were Bowe's trainers, not his babysitters. There was not really a person in Bowe's life outside of the ring that was keeping him in check. As a result, Andrew went from being a tune-up to much more. They underestimated what Andrew could do. They also overestimated what Bowe would be able to do. Andrew Golata, at his zenith, was a fearsome heavyweight. After being referenced by Main Events, Roger Bloodworth took a chance on Golota. Together they made considerable headway in the heavyweight division. Roger remembers his and Andrew's formative years:

**Roger Bloodworth:** Andrew came to me from Chicago. I was in Houston at the time and agreed to work with him on a flyer. Andrew was so athletic. He could have played in the NFL if he had chosen to do so. He was freakishly strong and had the speed to be effective with his power. He had only had twelve professional fights when he came into camp, but his physical talents were awesome. We had a couple fighters at various weights in the camp, and Andrew, the heavyweight, was the fastest sprinter we had. It seemed like we had a potential heavyweight champion on our hands. It seemed.

Andrew's tragic flaw was in his mental makeup. Deep within the recess of his soul was a demon that he did not have control off. It would rear its ugly head in times of high drama during his fights. Andrew had the pure boxing skills to subdue most of his opponents, but the few times he had to dig his feet in, bizarre happenings would be the result.

**Roger Bloodworth:** The Riddick Bowe fight was not the first time something happened that was unusual. A couple fights prior to that, we had fought Samson Po'uha. I had told Andrew before the fight that this guy looks fat (weighed in at 287 pounds before the fight and then rehydrated to God knows what), but don't underestimate him. Samson has good hand speed and can punch. Lo and behold, he tagged Andrew and was hurting him. Andrew weathered the storm but was being tested for the first time in his career. Andrew went on to blow Samson away in the fifth round. After the fight, Samson came up to me and told me, "Your man should not have hit me." At the time, I thought it was strange that he said that, but I would later found out that I had not heard him correctly. When we went back to watch the tape, we clearly saw Andrew bite him on the neck. He bit him so hard that he drew blood with a mouthpiece. Andrew became a little meaner after that fight. It actually made him better, but that fight put a chip on his shoulder. It let us know that anything was possible with Andrew.

**Sam Colonna:** I worked with Andrew from day one. I know him well and still know him well. Andrew is afraid of success. He has zero confidence in himself. He thinks everything will turn out bad for him, in part, because everything has. He does not know how to deal with attention. Whenever reporters would come around, Andrew would run and hide. He hated the spotlight. Andrew spoke English well and was a nice guy if you knew him, but when he would talk to the media, he would actually stutter. Attention just made him nervous.

Golota's mental block is something that could have been discovered if Rock Newman had committed to some type of scouting. There had also a nasty head butting incident on network television. Golota had fostered an unstable reputation in boxing circles, but for whatever reason, word did not seem to reach Rock Newman. They went ahead and made the fight. It was set for July 11, 1996. Since neither man held a major world title, selling the fight would be tricky. Kathy Duva, the present-day head honcho of Main Events Inc., was the publicist for the outfit before the tragic death of her beloved husband in 1996. At the time the fight was made, Main Events was in a period of transition. Kathy was taking over the organization while she was grieving. All of a sudden, she had a major heavyweight fight to promote.

**Kathy Duva:** When Dan passed, I had to take some time before taking full control of the reins. The first fight I was involved with when I came back was Andrew Golota-Riddick Bowe. I remember going to the press conference to announce the fight, thinking about how I was going to sell it. Riddick was no longer heavyweight champion and Andrew was a relative unknown. I knew the expectations would be low but somehow had to raise them. Dan had passed, and I knew that things like this came with the new job. I was slightly apprehensive about the promotion because of Rock Newman. He was difficult to work with at times. Everything about the fight would be a negotiation down to the posters. I knew at the time that taking on the responsibilities of staging the fight at Madison Square Garden, when the fight was not a guaranteed sell, was a pretty big risk. That's why we decided against copromoting the card. We let Bowe's camp control the event. In the back of my mind, I didn't think that Rock and his outfit truly had the administrative capacity to effectively promote an event at Madison Square Garden.

One thing would be assured the night of the fight, even if it were not a box office blockbuster. The crowd would be volatile. Polish boxing fans, to this day, might be the most underrated boxing fan bases in the world. They support their fighters like they would a football team. They sing and wave flags; it is not that much different from a national political convention. It's a social event. It's their chance to be ethnocentric. In Andrew Golota, the sizeable Polish population that occupied the tristate area finally had a relevant entity to cheer for. They came shouting and they were drunk. On the other side of the arena, were Brownsville's finest. More than a sample-sized portion of maybe the roughest ghetto in the city. To them, this was their home, their turf, and the arrogant Polish contingent had better respect that. While no one could have predicted the future, there were those in Golota's camp that believed Rock Newman was indirectly responsible for the antisocial personalities that infiltrated the Garden the night of the fight.

**Kathy Duva:** As I had predicted the fight was not selling a lot of tickets. The big room in Madison Square Garden can make a nice crowd look average. Rock Newman must have known this; we were told that he literally went to the Brownsville hood and passed out tickets the night before the fight. Many of the individuals who caused the chaos would not have been in the building if he had been a little smarter. Who knows who got their hands on tickets as the result of that?

# 24
# The Riot

**B**owe-Golota was a perfect storm for anarchy. The evidence was evident, but no one seemed to realize it until it was too late. Wayne Kelly was not among those that did not smell a little bit of danger. Wayne Kelly had been selected as the third man in the ring. His experience, and frankly his size (six foot four), made him an easy selection for the New York State Athletic Commission. Two big men with controversial résumés beget a big man to control them. Wayne Kelly was wary of the interesting history that both men seemed to posses. Uncanny happenings seemed to follow both men.

Wayne Kelly: **I had heard from several people that Andrew could get out of control late in fights. Everyone knew that Riddick and his camp could also fly off the handle at times. Going into the fight, I was a little nervous. I remember going into both dressing rooms and making it clear that I was not going to stand for any funny business. Riddick was his usual playful self. He nodded his head and went back to shadow boxing. Andrew, on the other hand, took a different approach. When I informed him of the consequences of unruly behavior, he looked at me and said, "I do what I have to do to win."**

The fight almost didn't take place. The day of the fight, Spencer Promotions pushed for the fight to be moved from a ten-round fight to a twelve-round fight. This caused some confusion because it seemed for a couple hours that the fight was not going to happen. After some back-and-forth, Golota agreed to the round change per added compensation. Spencer promotions paid Andrew an extra fifty grand to accept the stipulation, despite the lack of punctuality. Some boxing critics have wondered why Rock Newman would push for more rounds. It was clear at the weigh-in the day before that Riddick Bowe was not in the best of shape. He had also been inactive for eight months. The decision to lengthen the fight was incongruous at best. You're paying an extra fifty grand, and the stipulation could prove to be a disadvantage to your fighter. As the fans filed in, and the HBO lights flickered on, everyone seemed to realize that this fight would defy expectations. The first indicator was the intensity of the crowd. The Polish contingent surprised many with the passion and fury that they brought to the arena. Eastern Europe was in the house. Meanwhile, the Brownsville fans finally had a homecoming to attend. For whatever reason, Mike Tyson had yet to have a high-profile Garden homecoming. Riddick Bowe was finally giving them what they had been wanting for years. Riddick Bowe had fought Michael Dokes a couple years earlier at the Garden, but Dokes did not bring a soccer crowd with him. The confluence of these two agendas gave the event more electricity than anyone could have predicted. Another thing that no one could have foreseen was the technical mismatch that was about to take place.

**Roger Bloodworth: I had known Riddick Bowe since the amateurs, when he used to work with Lou Duva. He was a nice kid. I always liked him. I knew him and his style well. Because of that time with him, I knew we had a chance with Andrew. Andrew's jab was unlike anything Bowe had ever seen. It was snapping and accurate. Bowe had never really been jabbed before and I knew this would present him with problems. Andrew was ready too. During our final workout, I was doing mitts with him, and I could feel his power. It was intense. I knew we had a good chance to beat Bowe in that fight.**

Riddick Bowe was arguably in the worst shape of his career. After he defeated Evander Holyfield in the third fight, Riddick Bowe was forced to lay idle while Rock Newman gave birth to even more drama. Rock Newman sued Time Warner, and by extension HBO, after the third Holyfield fight, putting Riddick Bowe's career in temporary limbo. Riddick had been out of the gym for months. Riddick wasn't training, was overeating, and his body was deteriorating. Rock Newman had yet again made the decision to live in court with current business partners. Rock Newman did not exactly have a slam dunk of a case. The charges, while unspecific, were not seen as a big problem at HBO.

**Lou Dibella:** **It was a bullshit lawsuit. It never would have stood up if we had fought it. I remember Seth Abraham wanting to settle because we were in a business relationship with them. Seth believed it made no sense to carry on in court. I didn't want to settle because I was sure we could win, but in the end, we did.**

The lawsuit gave Riddick an unwanted, extremely long layoff. It eroded the momentum that he had created in defeating Holyfield and left him in a vulnerable place. He was overweight and not prepared to fight at a world-class level. Riddick Bowe was the type of fighter that needed to be in the gym; any type of extended vacation would lead him back to his bad habits. Sitting on the sideline for seemingly no reason, and unable to secure a big fight, Riddick Bowe became frustrated with the direction of his career. That frustration was evident to his handlers when everyone convened for training camp ahead of the Andrew Golota fight. When Riddick Bowe defeated Holyfield, he figured he would get a title shot, or maybe even a major fight, with Mike Tyson. No, instead he was taking a fight against a fighter he considered a bum. With everything that was on Riddick's mind, Andrew Golota became an afterthought. Riddick Bowe's attention deficit would have massive ramifications.

**Thell Torrence:** **It had not been a good training camp. Bowe had come into camp overweight. He also did not want that fight. He was more interested in going straight to Tyson, but Rock Newman convinced him and us that this was a better option. I thought the Tyson fight was next. Bowe was in the driver's seat for that fight. Camp did not begin well. Bowe simply did not want to be there. Camp took place in upstate New York in the middle of nowhere. After a couple days, Bowe left. He took off. He went home right in the middle of camp, leaving all of us hanging there for a couple of days. He came back eventually and camp resumed, but that lost time hurt**

us, no question. If my memory serves me correct, Riddick Bowe got in four good days of training for the fight. I think he figured the fight would not come off. He didn't want the fight. None of us did. We knew he had bitten Samson Po'uha. He had kicked another guy. Andrew Golota was a nut. We all figured he was on something. He was, however, well prepared to fight, no doubt about that.

Jim Lampley: First of all we were sure that Golota could give Bowe a challenge. I don't think that Riddick was totally on board with the fact that Golota was a problem. He could look slow on film. He was kind of a homely-looking presence in there. He had very heavy hands. There was no singular reason why; if he touched you, you felt it. We knew with his jab that he could be a problem for Riddick. It was just his mental disposition that could be his undoing.

The conditions were just right for an ass whupping. But not the ass whupping that the odds makers predicted. Andrew was a 20–1 underdog headed into the fight, according to Las Vegas odds makers and the New York bookies. The fight, televised live on HBO, was a barn burner from the word *go*. Bowe spent most of the early rounds trying to cope with the poking, dartlike jab of Golota. The shock of being jabbed by a man of comparable height took a couple of rounds to adjust too. Even when the technical adjustment was complete, Bowe was still getting tagged with clean effective right hands. Golota's confidence grew with each clean jab; he began to open up with accurate combinations, beating up Riddick Bowe. He was outboxing Bowe and outfoxing him. Golota was clearly the more athletic of the two and used his gifts to decimate Riddick Bowe's confidence over the first five rounds. The pro-Bowe crowd was reduced to stunned silence as Andrew teed off at will. It was a surprise to everyone how easily Andrew was winning the fight. No one thought it was possible for Andrew to last six rounds, let alone dominate. Riddick Bowe was among those that did not realize the gravity of his situation.

Larry Merchant: The first half of the fight clearly showed that Bowe had underestimated Golota, who was a big, strong, athletic fighter. There was a certain feeling before the fight that there were holes in Golota; we really did not know everything about him. There were a lot of boxing people that were skeptical of Golota. Riddick Bowe was the overwhelming favorite. I remember before the fight, Rock Newman was talking about putting a hole in his head with the jab, and then to everyone's surprise early in the fight, the jabber was getting outjabbed. This development told us that something was happening here. I knew early that this fight was going to be a little different than advertised.

As the punishment continued to mount, two things were clear, Andrew was the better fighter, and Riddick Bowe was not going to fold his tent. Riddick was taking a lot of punishment, but was still coming forward. He also was not going down or giving up. As the drama of the fight began to escalate, Andrew began his infamous regression. He began hitting Riddick well beneath the belt. At first it was seen as an accident, even the second time Wayne Kelly was lenient in his reprimand. No points were deducted. Roger Bloodworth, feeling shades of past fights, did what he could to prevent the inevitable.

**Roger Bloodworth:** A lot of people remember Lou Duva standing in the ring between rounds. Even though he was in the ring, I was actually the chief second. I would sit on the ring steps and give Andrew instructions. I explicitly remember telling Andrew no more body punches. He was hitting Riddick so easily that there was no reason to go to the body. Andrew simply did not listen to plain instructions. He just didn't have control of himself in times of stress.

Andrew was winning the fights on the cards in a wash. There was sufficient evidence to believe that he could have stopped Bowe in the late rounds if he continued to follow the game plan. The truth is none of that mattered. Andrew was not concerned with winning the fight. He simply wanted out of the situation completely. For the first time in Andrew's career, someone was taking his best shots and not quitting. It was most likely terrifying to a man who had gotten in boxing just to make a couple bucks. According to those close too him, he just wanted to live a mundane existence as a truck driver. There was nothing pedestrian about participating in a high stakes heavyweight fight that was becoming increasingly dangerous by the second.

Larry Merchant: Golota, in my mind at that point, was going to win the fight, but he mentally broke down. Mabye it was fatigue. Vince Lombardi used to say that fatigue makes cowards of us all. I think that may apply here, It was also frustration, both in the first fight and the second fight. Riddick Bowe was so tough in taking Andrew's best shots. Brutal, clean hard shots from a big strong athletic guy. Riddick Bowe, despite that, kept on coming. I believe that this eventually broke Andrew. Golota, for whatever reason—fatigue, frustration, his inability to control his emotions in the ring, Andrew—could not handle the pressure of competition. Fouling himself out was some combination of all that.

Riddick Bowe: You should have seen the look on his face. There was no emotion or feeling in his eyes. It was like he was somewhere else completely. It was also sudden. It came out of nowhere."

George Ward: I think that's just the way he fights. He was warned two times. He was going to win the fight. He was trying to go to the body too much. That's was his mistake. I don't think it was on purpose. The third time he did it, the Bowe people felt it was on purpose. Why would he do it on purpose when he was winning the fight? That's what makes it hard for me to believe that he was trying to hurt Bowe. He could have become champion of the world that night. He did it unintentionally. I was sitting ringside, and I did not see any spite or malice in his eyes.

**Jim Lampley:** We meet with our fighters the day before the fights. Andrew is an emotionally disturbed person. He was chronically depressed, short tempered, and low on self-esteem to be frank. People like that cannot go to the top of the mountain. Even over the course of a twelve-round fight. He had to blow it somehow, he had to tear it down. He was a body puncher; body punchers can get out of control, but this was different. This was a guy constantly, irrationally throwing low blows.

**Sam Colonna:** I knew deep down that Andrew had the best jab in the business. I just didn't realize he would handle Bowe that easily. It was very surprising. I think Andrew didn't know how to deal with the fact that he was going to win. He broke down mentally from all the pressure. I remember pleading with him to stop fouling, and he was somewhere else. His mind was somewhere else.

Andrew Golota proceeded to take matters into his own hands. He did not want to fight anymore; he was going to do anything to stop the situation from becoming any more dangerous than it already was. Seemingly without provocation, Andrew Golota hit Riddick beneath the belt repeatedly until he was disqualified. It was not just one punch either. It was combination punching beneath the belt. It was vicious and it incited the crowd. It was gasoline on a fire that was dying to spread. Wayne Kelly deducted two points after several warnings. Generally, if you have two points deducted, you risk being disqualified if you are docked a third point. Wayne Kelly defied conventional wisdom and allowed Andrew to continue, despite already having three points deducted.

**Bob Duffy:** Wyane Kelly did a great job. It's a credit to him that he did not call the fight after the third point. He saw that Andrew was clearly winning the fight and wanted to give him every opportunity to win. There was a lot on the line, and he recognized that. The problem was Andrew did not accept the gift.

After a lull in the action, following the third deduction, Andrew went to Riddick's balls again, pounding him with a low blow combination. Since Wayne Kelly was already well within his right to do so, and because he doubted that he could control Golota at that point, Wayne Kelly went ahead and made the responsible decision. Golota had shorted himself in every sense of the word. He was soundly beating a world-class fighter and seemed content to let it all go to waste. The night had begun with the shock of an apparent upset. It would now end with even more shock. All-time shock.

Wyane Kelly: He was fighting a heck of a fight. Low blows aside, Andrew did a masterful job that night. But what can I do? He is fouling repeatedly even though I am taking points from him. I told him as I best I could to stop or I would call the fight. He did not listen to me, and we got what we got. I have two jobs in there. The first one is to control the action if it gets out of hand. The second is to protect both men. Andrew was making my second job difficult, and I made a decision to protect one of the fighters. In this case, the fighter that needed protecting was Riddick Bowe. I stand by my decision.

Harold Lederman: It should be a judgment call to disqualify a fighter for fouls. Every situation is different. I have seen a referee disqualify guys after one warning. There is no hard-and-fast rule that you have to get rid of a guy after three fouls. There was no doubt about what to do when Mike Tyson bit Holyfield's ear off. The referee called the fight right there and then without warning. If the guy who got fouled is able to continue, a referee is more likely to not call the fight. People paid money to see a fight, and a referee understands that. Wayne was in a tough situation; millions of dollars were on the line. The winner would go on to bigger, better things. Golota, however, was so crazy that Wayne had no choice. The low blows were intentional and flagrant. Wayne did what he had to do to protect Riddick Bowe.

**Riddick Bowe:** He was winning the fight. I was a beaten man on that night, cuz. Andrew, because he is so fucking stupid, blew the fight. I am not sure if it was totally intentional, but it felt intentional. When someone does the same thing again and again, what am I supposed to think?

There was another drama unfolding in the Garden that night. This drama was not building in the ring; it was evolving in the stands. The Polish fans were cheering their hearts out for the surprising success that Andrew was having. Many of these Polish fans were Polish nationals. This was their chance to show their pride in a foreign territory, thousands of miles removed from Warsaw. The pro–Riddick Bowe crowd was disgruntled at the turn of events. The situation had potential to get ugly. As luck would have it, Madison Square Garden fumbled the responsibility of public safety.

**Larry Merchant:** It was a homecoming for Bowe, fighting in the Garden. His supporters attended it; he was the third guy to come from Brownsville, Brooklyn, after Floyd Patterson and Mike Tyson, to become heavyweight champion. Golota had many Polish supporters that were brandishing flags, cheering just like they do at soccer games. Given the shock of the event itself, the controversial ending of the event, it was not much of a surprise what ended up happening. There was back-and-forth in the stands throughout the course of the fight. Madison Square Garden was not ready to handle what happened, and as we saw, it got out of hand.

**Mackie Shilstone:** I remember getting to our seats and the atmosphere was intense, before the fight actually started. Any reasonable person would be a little unsettled by such an environment. The first instinct is to look for police officers. Some type of authority. I looked and looked and saw none. Given what was going on around me with the fans, that was a little disconcerting at the time, I must admit.

George Ward: Prior to that match, Madison Square Garden had made some cutbacks as it related to their security staff. Also, prior to that match, Madison Square Garden sparingly contracted NYPD to work its events. The guys that were assigned to that event were poorly trained and way too old to handle the type of individuals that were in the Garden that night. It was not a very good night for Madison Square Garden across the board. I am a commission inspector. I work for the State Athletic Commission. I am not actually an employee of the Garden, so I am not totally informed on why they made such a brainless decision.

At 2:35 of the seventh round, after being penalized three points, Andrew Golota was disqualified from his heavyweight tilt with Riddick Bowe. The crowd, which had been a character unto itself for most of the fight, went nuts as the decision was rendered. As Riddick Bowe lay in a heap on the mat, his entourage, buoyed by Rock Newman, followed Golota to his corner, shouting expletives and pointing fingers. Rock Newman stopped short of attacking Golota. Those with Rock, however, did not. Jason Harris, who had been involved in the Fan Man beat down, jumped right into the fray, bashing Andrew Golota with his walkie-talkie. At that moment, the smoldering fire that had been billowing for about two hours turned into a backdraft. Chaos erupted in Madison Square Garden. The ring that had housed just three men thirty seconds earlier was now full to the brim with individuals heavily vested in their respective fighter's interest. Some of the people in the ring could not care less who won the fight; they saw a chance to contribute to a spectacle and did so. The confusion in the ring was initially dismissed as a melee, something that would die down when the powers that be got their arms around the situation. What no one realized at the time was that no one powerful was in the building. The type of help that was needed would not be on its way for twenty minutes.

**George Ward:** I was working Riddick Bowe's corner that night. I saw someone from Riddick Bowe's camp (later identified by NYPD as Jason Harris) run across the ring and hit Golota with a radio or a cell phone or something. I was directly behind Golota when he was struck. At that moment, Golota's people jumped in the ring and went after Bowe's camp. I attempted to calm the situation down but was overrun by all the people that jumped into the ring. It was a racial brawl to be frank. Whites versus blacks. One hundred people jumped into the ring. I remember seeing Lou Duva lying on the ground, he was holding his chest. I moved him over to the side of the ring and stayed with him as a member of Golota's camp was literally draped over him. Once the paramedics grabbed Lou, I attempted to focus on getting people out of the ring. It was very difficult. I was wearing a gun that night. I was concerned that someone was going to grab it out of my holster and use it to hurt someone. I was a corrections officer at the time, so I am allowed by law to have my gun. This guy fighting that guy, it was chaos. I looked out into the stands, people ripping seats out, fighting for no reason. Polish people waving flags, just a massive scrap. All black versus white. The Garden security was useless. For a short time, we were truly helpless.

A slight majority of those in attendance were not actually participating in the riot; they were instead observing the viral madness that was taking place in front of their eyes. The situation went from contained to desperate in the blink of an eye. Eighty-year-old Lou Duva, a member of team Golota, was caught up in the explosion before he could react. Before the riot had even started, Lou Duva had been having issues with his heart over the course of the night.

Roger Bloodworth: A couple times during the fight, I noticed Lou clutching his chest. I would let him stand in the ring even though I was actually the chief second. Given his time in the sport, it was no problem, he had earned it. As he was climbing into the ring, we noticed he kept grabbing his chest. We knew of his heart problems and asked him if he could stay on the floor. We asked him to let me stand in the ring. Lou told me in colorful language that he was staying in the ring. We would find out later that his difibulator had been knocked out of place. When the riot broke out, his defibulator went, and he passed out right there on the mat. When the riot started, I jumped into the ring and started throwing punches. I grabbed someone from Bowe's camp, and we fell to the floor. Someone kicked me in the back of the head, and when I looked up, Lou was laid out; it was so scary. I then concentrated on getting him out of the ring.

Kathy Duva: When the riot broke out, we were moved rather quickly into the tunnel. In Madison Square Garden, the tunnels are not that far from the ringside seating, so we were lucky enough to be ushered out of danger. As I watched the craziness from afar, I noticed my father-in-law laid out on the mat. I went to go to him when a security official stopped me and told me it was too dangerous. Lucky for my family, they got a gurney to Lou and got him out of there. No way in the world I would have just sat there for too much longer with my eighty-year-old father-in-law laid out on the ring mat. I, along with my family, was escorted to the deeper reaches of the arena and met Lou at the ambulance that was set to take him to the hospital for observation. It was about as crazy a situation as I have ever seen. Fan Man was crazy, but there was not clear and present danger to

|                   | everyone in attendance. For this particular promotion, however, there was. |
|---|---|
| Thell Torrence:   | Absolute chaos. When the riot jumped off, it felt like forty people ran past me. At the time, the only thing I was concerned with was getting Eddie Futch to safety. Right before the last round of the fight, we sensed that something bad was going to happen. We decided to get our families out of there, which turned out to be a great decision. We also wanted to get Eddie out. Eddie was in his eighties and had no physical business being involved a potentially explosive situation. Much of what took place was a reaction. Our camp reacted to the fact that Golota was seemingly trying to hurt out fighter. What no one expected was the fans there supporting Golota to fight back. No one expected that. The absolute fury of the situation was breathtaking. Down in my office, I have a picture of me on the ring mat fighting attackers off. I was also worried about Lou Duva. I remember George Foreman's eyes getting as big as saucers. I followed George's eyes and noticed Lou Duva. I saw him laid out on the mat and did what I could to get him out of the ring. |
| Harold Lederman:  | It was havoc; there was people jumping over me to get in the ring. Fights galore, people were stepping on me and around me. I stayed behind George Foreman because I was sure that no one would mess with him. The scary part was that someone threw a two-by-four from the upper reaches of the arena; it came down with such force that it would have killed me if it had hit me. The piece of wood landed with a huge thud right on the table right in front of me, it was a scary moment. Jim Lampley's daughter was upstairs along with my daughter Judy in the mid- |

level seating. Jim ran up the stairs to remain close to them while reporting what was going on. It was total chaos around the ring. I didn't know where all these people came from.

Steve Farhood: That was nuts. I have never personally seen something like that at a fight. What I remember about that night was my wife freaking out because some friends of mine in England called and told her that there was a riot going on at Madison Square Garden. She knew I was there covering the fight. I get home, she was quite upset but happy to see me at the same time. I can't remember a crazier situation that I have been involved with personally

Bob Duffy: I remember the guy running across the ring and hitting Golota in the head, that's when everything got out of control. Before the fight started, people were already coming downstairs, but they had tickets for upstairs. When the riot exploded, people started running down the concourse after the fight, adding to the people already in the ring. Commission members went in the ring to try and break it up, but that became difficult because more and more people were overrunning the ring. People started throwing bottles, really just going crazy. I was all over the place. I was the chief inspector of the commission at the time; that meant I was, in essence, running the show. Golota was winning the fight and was in great shape. That was the surprising thing. I don't think Bowe was in shape. I think Wayne Kelly did a great job. I think he did an excellent job. Even though the commission was in charge of the event, we could not control what happened. The security at the garden was not good; a lot of our inspectors got hurt they got pelted just trying to do their job. I will say, that night though, that we had a top-flight team of inspectors. They did everything they could to help the situation. I was very proud of them that night; every inspector that was working that night stepped up to the plate. You could not have asked for a better group of inspectors.

Jim Lampley: I watched Jason Harris go across the ring and hit Andrew with an object that I could not identify at first. That's when all hell broke loose. I was sitting there, covering the melee from ringside. I saw one guy throw a chair; I then noticed that the fights were quickly spreading throughout the arena. I was standing there, watching the monitor, and Lou Duva looked dead. It appeared that he had fainted or expired. You had to observe the possibility that maybe Lou died on the spot because of his documented heart condition. Our table with audio gear was thrown to the floor. George Foreman was standing right behind me, forming a human barricade, protecting me as I was reporting. When the table went over, I thought, where the hell was the other microphone? I remembered there was one up the stairs on the second level. I dropped the ringside microphone and ran up the flight of stairs to continue the broadcast. Intrepid war reporter Larry Merchant decided to stay at ringside and report from the front. Many things contributed to things getting out of hand. Alcohol, the time of night—it was a lot things. We had been on air several minutes after the fight had ended. Ross Greenburg, in the truck, sent me a communication. He told me, "We are done covering this, make a personal comment and get us off the air." I had not even thought about the fact that my sixteen-year daughter was ringside. As soon as Ross said that, it hit me that my child was somewhere in the midst of all this. She turned out to be OK. We flew to Olympics in Atlanta the next day, and everyone on the train asked her, "You're the one, you're the daughter he was concerned about."

Ross Greenburg: It had only been a few years since Fan Man, and here we were again, unwittingly covering another crazy situation. We were in the truck, attempting to figure out what to do. The confusion was much like the Fan Man situation. As obtuse and absurd as it sounds, this had gone from a prizefight to a news story. I wanted to cover the story as best we could. I also wanted to make sure we kept the cameras rolling even after we went off the air. We were getting frantic calls back from ringside. We have this system where our commentators can talk to us without being heard on air. I was getting all types of calls from ringside. George Foreman was protecting everyone as best he could. I was very concerned about our staff and crew that were working ringside that night. Jim Lampley, thinking fast, knew that we had to broadcast the event in some way. He remembered that we had a microphone up the stairs in the scaffold and took off to go use it. For a while there, Jim didn't appear on the scaffold, and we were concerned about his safety. All of a sudden, he appeared and provided proper coverage of the madness. The shots of the Garden that night were amazing. Fights going on everywhere in the arena. At a certain point, I figured we have provided ample coverage and decided it was time to get off the air. I sent the transmission to Jim, and we concluded the broadcast. As we rolled the credits, those images of the fighting were not taped. They were *live* as the telecast came to an end. Never seen anything quite like that, not since Fan Man anyway.

If the riot had taken place in at the MGM Grand or even FedEx field in Maryland, one has to assume it would have been contained. Those venues employ police offers (and jail cells), making overtime as well as physically capable private security officials. It would have never become a riot. The most responsible party for the situation escalating to the point that it did was Madison Square Garden. For reasons that defy the laws of space and time, MSG did not feel it needed NYPD observing the event. They figured men eligible for Social Security would be more than enough to deal with potential problems that could arise. It was a colossal lapse in judgment by MSG officials. Their screwup was now being broadcasted to the world. Things went way beyond anyone's control when the fans gained access to the ring and the areas surrounding the ring. The only thing keeping these motivated young men from taking over the arena were geezerlike security officials appointed by Madison Square Garden. The lack of resistance gave the young men courage. There was a truly random pattern to the riot. It died down in some areas and then flared up again. Larry Merchant, one of the very brave souls that stood within the riot, seemed unconcerned with his personal safety. Larry transitioned from calling the fight to calling the riot rather seamlessly. It was not much different from Geraldo reporting the war on location.

**Larry Merchant:** I had been ringside at a previous riot at the previous Madison Square Garden, in the mid- to late sixties; it was Carlos Ortiz vs. Ismael Laguna. The fans were very unhappy with the decision and started to throw things at the ring from the upper deck. Some of the obstacles were empty beer and liquor bottles. While a lot of people dove for cover, I was dumb enough to just stand there and look. It had been quite a sight to see glass bottles being hurled from all directions five hundred feet above you. I would suppose that experience numbed me to the chaos that night at the Garden. When the Bowe-Golota riot touched off, I remember figuring there wasn't a bullet with my name on it, or so I hoped! I figured it could not be more dangerous than the first riot I had seen at the Garden. I simply did not think anybody was coming after me. I hadn't done anything. The scene looked chaotic but did not seem particularly dangerous, it probably was more dangerous than I realized in retrospect. I know Jim Lampley went to an elevated position to report for our network. I just reported it, as it was as I saw it. I had not seen such an upheaval coming. There had been no history of such an event for either fighter's contingent. We could see there was a lot of passionate fans wearing red and waving Polish flags. No one saw the potentially volatile mix. Bowe coming from Brooklyn brought fans of his elk to the party and we got what we got. We just didn't expect it. Of course Madison Square Garden didn't either. Their primary security forces were not in attendance. I don't know if I heard correctly, but I heard it might have been a labor situation or a strike.

# 25
# NYPD

In an age of 911, and Homeland Security, a riot in the center of New York City would have been contained on sight; the response would have taken place quickly. On this night, however, it took time. That's amazing considering the prime location of the venue. Madison Square Garden is literally in the center of Manhattan. It makes you wonder what the police were actually doing at the time of the riot. It was well known that a fight was taking place. With fights come unruly fans. Even though Madison Square Garden informed NYPD they would not need their services, it's hard to believe that city cops were not at least staking the joint out. NYPD would arrive on the scene some twenty minutes after the riot jumped off. By the time the cops and their horses entered Madison Square Garden, the energy in the building was frenetic. Roger Bloodworth had a panoramic view of the police entering the building.

**Roger Bloodworth:** I had been kept in the ring during the riot. The MSG officials told me that leaving the ring with a Golota jacket on was most likely not the best idea. The riot was everywhere in the building. It would start and stop and start up again. No one was safe, whether they were fighting or not. I saw a man sitting on a chair just watching; someone ran up behind him and hit him with a chair. It was like something out of the WWE. A couple moments later, the police rolled in. It was not uniformed cops. It was the riot police all geared up. The entrance was spectacular. They knew what they were doing, super professional and efficient. They took control right away; everyone seemed to calm down in the face of machine guns and tear gas.

NYPD seemed to have two goals during their raid on Madison Square Garden. They wanted to gain control, and did so upon arrival. They also wanted to get the fighters and their handlers out of the building right away. Everyone has a different story about his or her respective police escort out of the building.

**Mackie Shilstone:** We have been in the dressing room during most of the riot, waiting around to see what was going to happen. Riddick actually did not get back to the dressing room right away. For a while it was I, his wife, and some other people in the entourage. It was scary for a while there because of the unknown, of where this situation was going. After Riddick came back with some commission members, the police finally came and got all of us about a half hour after everything took place. They formed a phalanx around us like the movie *300* and herded us out of the building. When we got outside, we were in for another shock. I would find out later they blocked off streets surrounding the building, but I did not know at that time. The streets were dead silent; there was no one outside except for police. We were at the center of New York City on Saturday night, and there was not a peep. It was chilling.

**Roger Bloodworth:** We were back in the dressing room, attempting to calm Andrew down. He was pissed. I remember Rudy Giuliani walking into the dressing room and apologizing to us. We told him it was it not his fault, he said, "Yeah, but it's my city." After Rudy left, we turned our attention back to Andrew. He had been cut on the back of his head by the walkie-talkie and was bleeding down his neck. We told him we were going to take him to the hospital because he needed stitches. We could actually do the stitches ourselves, but we did not have any type of local anesthetic. Andrew looked at us, put his head forward, and said, "Do it," and we did, stitches without any type of drugs. Gosh he was tough. The cops walked in while we were lacing Andrew up and told us they wanted to get us out of there. We got our things together and headed for the exit under heavy police scrutiny. During the walk, Andrew convinced one of the cops to give him a nightstick; it was funny because Andrew would not give it back. I think he autographed it and sent it back. It was clear that Andrew felt he was in danger until he left the city. We were loaded into this big police truck and taken back to the hotel.

Bob Duffy: The NYPD had a policy at the time; they don't want the cops going into any building or venue that housed a sporting event. I was a cop for twenty-five years before I worked for the commission. I remember not being allowed in Shea Stadium. NYPD feel that the responsibility of the event is the venues. Why did they take so long to get to the Garden? I don't know. Maybe the guys back at the station didn't want the cops on sight to go in right away. I have to imagine that NYPD realized the situation was a little bigger than just an everyday street fight. It takes time to put a task force together. It's not like they could send ten cops and that would be enough. They needed at least one hundred cops to deal with the situation I saw. It makes some sense that it took more time than usual. They were prepping.

George Ward: NYPD came in at DEFCON 3. They came in on horses and in riot gear. They came hard and they came fast. It's amazing the peacefulness that came over the place when the cops arrived; they dispersed the crowd with ease, 150 riot cops with helmets and batons. At that moment, I finally had some leverage to clear the ring. I cleared the ring. I was with Riddick Bowe throughout the entire riot. Bowe was concerned about his wife. He had not seen her since the fighting started. He lost it a little bit. He was looking for her, he was screaming her name, "Judy, Judy, where are you." He lost it. He was going berserk. I suggested to him that we go back to the dressing room to see if she was there. He agreed, and off we went. His homeboys and handlers surrounded us. We fought our way through the crowd and made it to his dressing room in one piece. His wife and his children were in the dressing room, much to Bowe's relief. She was crying. I remember seeing Bowe consoling her as I closed the door.

Riddick Bowe: I was worried about my family at first, but they were taken out, and everyone was OK. I remember sitting in the dressing room just embarrassed. I could not believe this bum did to me what I was supposed to do to him. The cops were cool. They were on a gangsta tip. It was not a game to them when they took my people and me up out of there. They kept us safe and I appreciate that.

Derek Gionta: One of the most bizarre and disappointing scenes in boxing history. Golota probably would have won the fight and was controlling the seventh round with his jab. Then he gets a third point deducted for low blows, yet he still managed to throw a couple more obvious low blows, the latter of the two causing Bowe to fall on his back and referee Wayne Kelly to stop the fight. The riot capped off a terrible night for the sport.

Larry Merchant: I remember thinking that night as I was leaving in the arena that I would not mind seeing those two fight again.

Shortly after the fight, Thom Loverro, who had covered the event, wrote in the *Washington Times*

> **At Madison Square Garden on Thursday night, the privilege of sitting in the press area turned into a curse. After the riot began in the ring at the Riddick Bowe-Andrew Golota fight, which ended abruptly in the seventh round when Golota was disqualified for repeated low blows, we all watched intently from our special seats just a few feet from the action, trying to figure out who was hitting whom in the chaos before us.**
>
> **But the fighting spilled out of the ring and then in front of us. I turned around to see fights breaking out all over the crowd, with those skirmishes getting closer to the ring. Fans were jumping over the barrier dividing the press seats from the rest of the arena, turning over tables, tossing chairs aside.**
>
> **We then turned from observers to survivors, trying to find shelter. There was none. For once, I was wishing we were sitting up in the cheap seats.**

The Riot at Madison Square Garden was a disaster of the highest order. It was a black mark on boxing and to the city of New York at the same time. Human nature can be visually stunning to behold, this riot, this temporary war zone, was about as graphic as human nature gets. One thing was for sure. The City of New York was going to seek justice. When the riot ended and the last chair had been thrown, NYPD was still on sight conducting its investigation. The investigation would go all night and into the morning. The following day, a number of people were summoned to police headquarters in Manhattan to give a statement. Some of the parties summoned were asked to identify potential suspects. The full weight of city hall was upon the NYPD; they were in a position where they had to hold folks accountable. Rudy Giuliani wanted New Yorkers to wake up the next morning and see that the city was already pursing suspects.

**Kathy Duva:** I remember being called in to police headquarters in the wee hours of the morning. I was just asked some basic questions and sent on my way. I remember thinking how relieved I was that we chose not to copromote the card. Not having to deal with all of the liability and the city's investigation of the incident was nice. I got home at like eight in the morning; my kids were eating cereal asking me where I had been. It was a crazy night.

Lou Dibella: It's amazing that no one was killed. I thought for sure someone was going to get stabbed or shot. The next morning, I was sitting there with Rudy Giuliani and the police commissioner indentifying people on the tape. The situation was actually started by Rock Newman and company. I remember one of Bowe's people using that walkie-talkie and then all hell broke loose. I was sitting ringside with Rudy and some other people that night. It was nuts.

The fallout from the riot was considerable. The New York State Athletic Commission, under the watchful eye of city hall, took action against Riddick Bowe and his handlers. What was confusing about their agenda is that it seemed to blame Riddick Bowe for the riot even though he had been the fighter who was chronically fouled.

Thell Torrence: We didn't understand that. This man really hurt Bowe. He did it illegally to the point where the referee disqualified him. So everyone blames Bowe? If Bowe had done that, they would have taken him to jail. I still don't understand why New York City, Bowe's hometown, blamed him? He was the one that was fouled!

Andrew Golota, for whatever reason, was absolved of wrongdoing even though his actions touched off the entire situation. The City of New York pointed a big finger at the New Yorker and let Golota walk away, check in hand.

Riddick Bowe: I thought it was racial. How am I getting blamed for everything? I didn't do anything wrong. I was one the lying down on the ring mat on the other side of the ring from everything when it started. It made no sense.

The state commission of New York withheld one million of Riddick's purse pending an official investigation. They also fined Spencer Promotions $250,000 and suspended Rock Newman. Rock Newman was also suspended from Madison Square Garden for the foreseeable future. Some believed that Rock Newman incited the riot. That may not be true.

**Thell Torrence:** We were in the dressing room after the riot. Benard (Brooks) came up to me and told me, "I think I started that whole thing." Some people point to Rock Newman and Jason Harris. Truth is, no one knows who actually started it. We just know that Bowe was fouled. Horribly fouled.

Lou Duva was publicly critical of Newman in the wake of the incident. Lou had been hospitalized the night of the fight. Thankfully, he had since been updated to stable condition. Lou Duva pointed out that Rock did not even go to check on Riddick when the fight was stopped; he instead went right after Andrew Golota. The legal ramifications would be civil and criminal in nature. Three men, from Brooklyn no less, sued Madison Square Garden, Riddick Bowe, Rock Newman, and Spencer Promotions for injuries suffered the night of the fight. Andrew Golota and his trainer, Sam Colonna, would get in on the act in January of 1997, suing Riddick Bowe and Rock Newman for an unspecified amount of damages, rumored to be in the millions. They charged Spencer Promotions with causing them physical pain and stress the night of the riot.

**Sam Colonna:** Rock Newman is responsible for the entire situation. He is the one that initially charged Andrew; it is Rock Newman that got other people involved. I did sue them. I believed that the situation was their fault, and I still believe that. There was no reason for the situation to become what it was. I was never a fan of Rock Newman anyway. The way he carried himself in a couple different situations was unacceptable. After the first Holyfield fight, he beat up

> some photographer that was just trying to do his job. He is the one who should have worn gloves and got in the ring, know what I mean?

Criminally, NYPD would have the last laugh. The police department arrested sixteen people for their role in the disturbance. Mr. Mayor promised the inquiring public that everyone involved would be punished and followed that course of action to a tee. For whatever reason, Riddick Bowe was in city hall's crosshairs. The city held Riddick Bowe responsible. They gave Andrew Golota a pass. No fines or suspensions, no type of censure, nothing for Mr. Golota. Mr. Mayor was a wonderful man, a hero, but not holding Andrew Golota accountable in any way shape or form was unacceptable. It was even more shameful to wrongly assign blame to an athlete indigenous to the tristate area. State supreme court justice, Louis York, made note of this flawed mind-set. Judge York threw out a complaint filed against Bowe in the wake of the riot. In his decision to dismiss the suit he wrote,

> **It is laughable to assume that lying prostrate on the ground, groaning and dazed from intense pain, RiddickBowe was in a position to incite anyone to riot, there is no common law duty for a prize fighter, a manager or a promoter to protect against injury during a riot at a prize fighting event.**

# 26
# Chaos Redux

The mainstream attention that Bowe-Golota received in the wake of the fight was considerable. It was the lead on SportsCenter and other sports ticker shows. As violent and dangerous as the riot had been, it gave the fight quite a bit of notoriety. Certainly more than many observers thought was possible going in. The business of boxing dictates that there is no shame in going back to the same well, if the public demands it. The public was interested for two reasons: They wanted to see if there would be another riot, and they also wanted to see if the first fight had been a phenomenon. Was Golota that much better than Bowe? The two sides did not waste any time figuring out the details. HBO, realizing the intrigue of a return match, pushed for the two sides to come to some type of agreement. HBO also gave Andrew some incentive.

**Roger Bloodworth:** HBO offered Andrew a lot of money should he win. A lot of money. They were surprised and impressed by the first fight. There was a lot riding on the fight for Andrew, and it was a fight he could win.

**Kathy Duva:** We were the copromoter of the second fight, which took place in Atlantic City, but my brother-in-law and attorney made the deals with HBO, Rock, and Atlantic City. I was simply involved in marketing the fight. Looking back, we had Arturo Gatti *and* Hector Camacho on that card. What a show. That could never happen in the present world of boxing. I am sure I was not too interested in promoting the second fight because of the difficulty of dealing with Rock Newman. My husband had died a couple months earlier; the first fight had been a disaster. I didn't need the stress and handed off the second fight to other members of my family.

There were whispers of steroids coming out of Bowe's camp. At first they were just rumors, but as the weeks began to go by, they became full-blown accusations. Bowe and company believed that's the only way Andrew could have competed at the level he did. No one knows for sure, but there was a feeling in Bowe's camp that Andrew's strange behavior and scary strength seemed unnatural. Rock Newman made sure that the second fight would be played on an even playing field.

**Roger Bloodworth:** Riddick Bowe's people convinced him that Andrew was on steroids, so they worked random drug testing into the contract. As far as I know, Andrew never used performance-enhancing drugs, and the test all came back clean. I remember the drug testers coming into camp twice, twice they didn't find anything. Riddick Bowe and fans have used roids as an excuse, even to this day, but Andrew Golota was tested and came back clean. Say what you want, but he came back clean.

Many fans have wondered about the possibility of Andrew using steroids during his fights with Bowe, and possibly before. Since he appeared to be clean in the lead up, claiming he was on drugs would not be a valid excuse the second time around. Riddick Bowe had been battered and outboxed in the first fight. He had been outclassed for the first time in his career. The burden of proof was on Riddick Bowe. He knew that he had something to prove to the world. The public accusations about his work ethic had plagued him throughout his career. The fact that he came in at almost three hundred pounds when he arrived at training camp put his career on the brink of disaster. Andrew Golota would have Riddick Bowe's earning potential in the palm of his hand come fight night. Some have argued the logic in taking the second fight for Bowe. Why take on such dangerous opponent that outclassed you the last time out, and fouled you chronically? What was the upside? Pursing a second fight after the events of the first again calls the matchmaking abilities of Rock Newman into question.

**Jim Lampley:** You certainly understand the sales value of a rematch. When the first fight boasted a highly controversial ending. Riddick was always very confident, he was sure he was the better guy. If Eddie Futch does not prevent you from taking the second fight, I am not sure who does. Eddie was the most protective and humane of all the trainers that worked with heavyweights. I don't doubt for a second it was the biggest money fight out there for Riddick. Rock Newman and his never-ending ego trip, however, could prevail over any conventional wisdom, even the great Eddie Futch.

Riddick Bowe's life and career was in a downward spiral. Just when things could not get any worse, they did. Eddie Futch, Bowe's long-time trainer, stepped down before Riddick's rematch with Andrew Golota. Some have speculated that differences over matchmaking, money, and the direction of Riddick's career influenced the decision. No one knows for sure.

**Thell Torrence: Things had gotten pretty bad at that point. Eddie was angry about some things that were going on. I cannot be sure. But I believe money had something to do with it. I was so close with Eddie. I had been calling him, and he was not answering his phone. I went over to his house to make sure he was all right. When I got there, he told me he would not be working the fight. I didn't want to work at first. When he told me he was done, I didn't know what to think. I didn't want to work the fight at first. Shortly after that, Rock called me and asked me if I would work the fight. I had never made a major payday with those guys, and I took the opportunity. I also hated the thought of leaving Bowe. I wanted Eddie there, but I could not abandon Riddick. Our training camp was in New Jersey for the second Golota fight. I had Montell Griffin, Riddick Bowe, and James Toney. Things were great at first. Riddick was at a good weight, right on target. I had to leave to work Montell's fight. I told Kareem and Vernon to not overwork him. I didn't want Bowe to be drained, to be sapped of his strength. I**

**came back, and he was so thin, so off target. I could not believe it. Weight has to taper off. Heavyweights have to retain some of their strength. I knew we were going to have a problem.**

The second fight was staged in Atlantic City, New Jersey, on December 14, 1996. The turnaround for the fight seemed swift. Rematches all seem to have a life of their own. Some rematches like Pavlik-Taylor were made right away, rematches like Marquez-Pacquaio or Hearns-Leonard took years to make. The haste of the scheduling gave the impression to many that there was finally a sense of urgency in Bowe's camp. Golota had set Riddick Bowe's career back; this served to motivate Riddick. Bowe confirmed public perception, weighing in at a ready to order 235 pounds. It was seventeen pounds lighter than he had clocked in at six months earlier, his appearance looked much trimmer than the body he had sported in July. Riddick Bowe, despite being outclassed in the first fight, was a 3-1 favorite according to the oddmakers.

**Roger Bloodworth:** Riddick came up to me before the fight and told me, "I'm going to whup your boy's ass slim." I told him, "Yeah right." I knew the fight was in the bag. Andrew was simply the better fighter at that point. The only thing that could derail us was Andrew's temperament when the going got rough. It was in the back of my mind, but we had really focused on hitting above the belt in camp. I actually didn't think it was possible that it would happen again.

**Harold Lederman:** I went into the second fight thinking that Golota was so crazy that no one knew what to expect. Lou Duva kept defending him, but I kept saying to myself that anything could happen with someone this unhinged. He could have been a great fighter with all that ability when he was young, but no one really understood what his problem was. I never really understood Golota. Bowe should have walked away from him after the first fight. Knowing he was that screwy and dangerous to me raises questions about what exactly Bowe's handlers were thinking when they agreed to make the second fight.

**Sam Colonna:** We spent the entire camp telling Andrew to stay away from body punches. We even put a pair of trunks on the heavy bag. Every sparring session, workout, or run, we told Andrew to keep his punches above the belt. We knew, however, that if he broke down mentally, he would revert back to fouling. We just hoped it would not come to that.

**Thell Torrence:** I didn't want the fight. I didn't want it for so many reasons. I did not control things. I didn't make those decisions. But Andrew Golota has problems. He really hurt Riddick in the first fight. He was a dangerous guy. Bowe was never the same after fighting that guy.

The two fighters that shocked the boxing world with the intensity of the first fight were back again to stage an encore. Both men were flawed in their own way, that's what made them riveting to watch. Many believed that the riot had just been a freakish occurrence. Many also believed that the low blows that precipitated the riot were another freakish occurrence that could not possibly happen again. What would take place on that night was just as brutal, and even more head-scratching than the first act of the fistic epic.

Andrew Golota showed up to fight. He displayed even fiercer ring generalship than he had in the first encounter. He was moving side to side too but standing his ground when he had to. The first two rounds were a nasty boxer/puncher tutorial. Andrew Golota was the professor. As much punishment as Bowe had taken in the first fight, Riddick had not actually tasted the canvas. Andrew wobbled him but was unable to put Bowe on his butt. Golota, with his combination punching and movement, had Bowe stumbling all over the ring. Andrew finally got Riddick Bowe on the ground in the second round. A right hand to the temple followed by a blind left to the forehead led to a delayed reaction knockdown. It was only the second time in Riddick's entire career that he had been knocked down. Lost in Golota's second round assault was a foul that was just as egregious as a low blow. After the knockdown, a wobbly Riddick Bowe displayed tremendous valor, exchanging with Golota even though he was hurt. He was attempting to fight fire with fire, and it must have been discouraging to Golota. He hits this man with his Sunday punches, and the man gets up and fights harder. As they were in close quarters, Golota shot a WWE head butt and connected, cutting himself. Eddie Cotton wasted no time letting everyone know who was in charge. He deducted a point from Golota on sight. There was no question about the intention of the head butt. HBO replays, played in between rounds, had Andrew dead to rights. Andrew put himself in Eddie Cotton's crosshairs seemingly right away. Eddie must have realized at that moment that all the rumors were true. Andrew Golota and his brief reactive psychosis were as advertised. Andrew Golota entered the fight with little room for error. When he committed that first foul, his margin for error grew even slimmer.

Despite the foul, Golota dominated the action in the second and continued to command the ring for most of the third round. Bowe seemed rejuvenated in the fourth round, finally laying some wood to Golota. Bowe landed one of his roundhouse right hands, stunning Golota. After a barrage of punches, Riddick sent Golota to the canvas for the first time in his career. Golota rose to his feet with blood streaming down his face and took the standing eight-count. Andrew took the full eight seconds and agreed to resume the combat. Golota advanced back into the inferno; he took a powerhouse uppercut and a barrage of hooks. Golota was hurt, he was bleeding, and he was getting beat up. It was at this point that Andrew reverted to his Madison Square Garden roots. When Bowe began to slow down, Golota bodied him into the ropes and threw low blow combinations. All eyes shifted to the third man in the ring. To Eddie Cotton's credit, he let Golota get away with a couple of low blows before he actually made an issue of it. It appeared that Cotton wanted to avoid a disqualification. After the initial warning, Golota dropped another low blow combination that sent a helpless Bowe to the canvas, clutching his genitals. The crowd was in a stunned silence. Andrew was doing it yet again. Maybe he did it to get out of trouble; perhaps this was the beginning of him breaking mentally. Andrew had known before the fight it was going to be tough. There had been reports that he was distraught in his dressing room prior to the fight.

**Larry Merchant:** I do recall there was some type of personal weirdness chaos going on in Golota's dressing room before the fight. There was an indication that night of tension and nerves coming out of Golota's dressing room. The fight was the fight. We know what happened. Bowe took tremendous punishment and kept on coming, which again broke Golota. He could not deal with that. It broke him spiritually and emotionally, and he reverted to doing what he did in the first fight. When Bowe came back from the second-round knockdown to cut Andrew and knock him down, it seemed to be a big blow to Andrew emotionally, and as we saw, that was the beginning of the end.

**Roger Bloodworth:** If you watch the original telecast, you can see me going nuts between rounds four and five. I was shouting in his ear, "No more body punches." I told him to snap the jab and throw *no* more body punches. He was sitting there, but it seemed like his mind was elsewhere. You could hear me yelling that Bowe was shot. He was. He looked weak and lethargic in the ring.

Andrew took the advice of his corner and focused on punching above the chest. It paid dividends in the very next round. Bowe found himself backed up under fire from Andrew's free-flowing combinations. The punishment lasted the entire round. Midway through the round, Andrew landed two straight right hands that blew Bowe's head back so far, he could have seen the crowd behind him. Bowe then slouched forward and was met with pinpoint bodypunching. He fell to his knees, clutching Andrews's feet. Bowe was as hurt as he had ever been in his career. He bravely rose to his feet and was unsteady. Eddie asked him if he wanted to continue. If Eddie had stopped the fight, no one would have objected. Eddie chose not to call the fight and allowed Riddick to continue. Andrew then battered Riddick, who was using the ropes just to stay on his feet. Golota thrashed Riddick right up to the sound of the bell, punctuating the assault with a left-right combination that bent Bowe's head back twice. It had been an awful round for Riddick Bowe.

Andrew landed fifty-six power punches to Bowe's seventeen. Bowe appeared to be a beaten man. Many have wondered why they didn't stop the fight. Bowe had earned a reputation as a valiant warrior that could take a fighter's best and come right back. This reputation was earning him more time. The fifth round saw the action temper a couple notches, but the punishment still remained. Andrew, content to fight from distance, peppered Bowe with the jab. Moving him every time it landed. Riddick Bowe was unsteady on his feet. He continued to stand in and take copious amounts of punches. At some point in the round, Bowe seemed to find a reserve of energy. He began pressing the action, backing up Golota with looping right hands. The punches had a long arc and were easy to see. Golota was cognizant of Bowe's power at this point. Andrew was not about to get reckless even though he had the upper hand in the fight. The two men began exchanging, which was amazing considering the dire straits Bowe had been in just three minutes earlier. It was a commendable display of courage from both fighters as they both dug their feet in, much to the delight of those in attendance at Boardwalk Hall. It was electrifying theater. Larry Merchant, live on air for HBO, made a prophetic statement to the viewers at home at the end of round five.

**"Even if Riddick Bowe goes on to win this fight, his career as a top flight heavyweight may be over because of all the punishment he is taking tonight."**

Bowe was breathing heavy. He was taking power punches and was seemingly out of the fight. The result of the fight seemed academic to everyone not named Riddick Bowe. He refused to give in; it ended up being to his detriment. Riddick Bowe had nothing left physically. All that was left was his incredible heart. All the questions about the size of his heart were being answered now, in this fight, but with a price. Bowe managed to exchange with Golota in spurts, but it was clear that Riddick Bowe was a spent force. Barring a miracle, Bowe would be knocked out if the fight went much longer. At the end of the seventh round, a very telling moment took place. Eddie Cotton, obviously concerned about Bowe, put his arm around Riddick's waist and guided him to his corner. That raised questions about Eddie Cotton after the fight. If the fighter does not have the wits to walk back to his corner, under his own strength, how in the world should be allowed to continue? Andrew Golota threw seventy-six punches and landed fifty-six in the round. That's an unheard-of connect percentage. He was also throwing power punches, doing unknown amounts of damage to Bowe physically. Thell Torrence, who was the chief second for Bowe's corner that night, knew that the end of the fight was near for his fighter either way.

**Thell Torrence:** **I was giving him instructions, but he did not seem to hear me. He seemed out of it. His eyes were glassy, and he seemed punch drunk. I had never seen that look on Riddick's face before. It was sad and scary at the same time. That beating was taking more from him than we realized. After the seventh round, I told him I was going to stop the fight if he did not do something to change what was happening.**

Bowe was at the point where his own right hands were knocking him off balance. He managed to land one meaningful combination in round eight. The stronger, fresher fighter was still trouncing him. As the bell for the ninth round sounded, Riddick Bowe took one deep breath and got off his stool for the last meaningful round of his career.

As one sided as the beating had been, Bowe yet again showed a willingness to trade in the ninth round. He was backed up on the ropes but was throwing and slipping. It was his most positive round since the middle of the fight. Golota was landing punches but seemed to be slowing down. Bowe's refusal to give in was frustrating Golota. The frustration was about to boil over. Riddick Bowe, having spent the first minute of the round on the ropes, landed a huge counter right that hurt Golota and caused him to move back toward the center of the ring. Bowe followed him, leaned on him, and kept punching. Golota, as he did in the fourth round, responded to trouble by throwing low blows. The first couple low blows were let go by Eddie Cotton. The persistence and the severity of the fouls, however, led him to make the tough decision. As Bowe retreated a couple of steps back from the action, Golota jumped forward and landed a three-punch low-blow combination. Eddie Cotton had officially had it. He walked Andrew over to a neutral corner and called the fight at 2:53 of the ninth round. The silence in Boardwalk Hall was deafening. No one could believe that Golota had yet again thrown away an easy victory. A victory that would have qualified as a marquee progression.

Roger Bloodworth: I was in shock when they stopped the fight. I could not believe it happened to us again. We were hurting Bowe, really beating him up, and to think that we had just given away a second fight to this guy drove me nuts. I didn't know what to make of it. Andrew had a hard time dealing with adversity, and even though he was winning the fight, he was clearly dealing with adversity. I was disappointed because we had spent a good amount of time in training camp trying to avoid this very situation.

Kathy Duva: I could not believe it happened again. I was in shock for most of the night. We were winning the fight and gave it away yet again. It was not comical, but it had a "comedy of errors" feel to it. I will never forget sitting in a coffeeshop with Roger Bloodworth until the sun came up in total shock over what happened. We could not believe it.

Riddick Bowe: He had the fight won. He did it to me again. And yet again, because he was an idiot, he could not control himself. Maybe it wasn't the roids. Maybe he just could not handle me not going away. Whatever the case may be, he put a hurt on me that night physically and mentally. I can't explain how it felt. It was the saddest night of my career

Thell Torrence: The low blows took his spirit. It was painful to watch because I loved Bowe. The low blows are what took it out of him. Riddick gets zero credit for continuing to fight while he was in pain. People don't understand how badly low blows hurt.

It takes everything out of you. And this was combination punching, again and again. It's unacceptable.

The crowd seemed to be waiting for another riot to jump off. It never happened. A duly educated New Jersey State Control Board in cooperation with the Atlantic City Police force had secured the arena in the event of any shenanigans. There would be no riot on this night. Before the fight, the powers that be had limited credentials, cut down on the size of the fighters entourages, and packed the arena with security guards and cops. The story after the fight was the physical health of Riddick Bowe. Sometimes after a prizefight, combatants will literally have to lick their wounds before rejoining society. Cuts and swelling happen frequently and worsen after the fight. These types of injuries are fixable with time and proper care. Brain injury, however, knows no cure and has everlasting effects.

**Roger Bloodworth:** Many people think that Riddick was shot in the second fight and that's why he lost. That's incorrect. He was in good shape and in a good state of the mind before that fight. I had known Riddick for years; from what I could tell, he was just fine before the fight. What is telling to me is before the fight he had made that playful remark to me about beating Andrew in that familiar gentle giant voice. After the fight, however, he came up to me and attempted to tell me, "Hell of a job." Riddick could not even put the words together. He had gone from perfect diction to punch drunk in one fight. That's when I knew for sure that he was done as a prizefighter. He had taken a tremendous beating and was already showing serious signs of brain injury.

**Larry Merchant:** I don't remember Bowe before the fight. I remember Bowe seeming damaged after the fight. Going all those rounds with Holyfield, two killer fights with Andrew. It was sad to watch because the guy was very likable. He was fun to be around.

He loved being champion. He liked to play to the cameras, related to the media well. There were subtle clues that he was a little slower directly after the fight. It usually does not show up that way right away. It happens down the road. It didn't seem like a shock that his career ended so fast after seeing him that night. I do remember that he was showing in hindsight the early signs of pugilistic dementia. You could not know that at the time. It could have been a guy that had been in a tough fight that was still not fully coherent. I cannot say I have seen that, and it actually turned out to not be the beginning of the end, but the end of the end.

Riddick Bowe: I didn't think I was done. I felt a little woozy after the fight but not to the point where retirement was an option. People can say what they want; Andrew Golota did not end my career. After the Golota fight, I had choices to make. At the time I just wanted to make the right one. I knew at the time that a change was going to be made one way or the other.

Thell Torrence: I was there in the locker room. There was no talk of retirement. It had been a tough fight. Riddick was upset, but he seemed OK. I didn't see anything that seemed out of the ordinary. Some people say he didn't seem the same. I personally didn't see anything wrong with him.

# HBO

The end of Riddick Bowe's career as a top-level prizefighter would be as abrupt as anyone could have imagined. In the wake of the brutality of his fights with Golota and Holyfield, many were concerned about his physical health. Some in the boxing community were speculating that Riddick Bowe was suffering from brain damage at the age of twenty-nine. There was speculation that Riddick Bowe's legs and his reflexes had come and gone. When a fighter reaches the point where his long-term health is at risk, it falls upon those around him to urge him to retire. Riddick Bowe was urged by those around him to retire from the sport of boxing. HBO was among those that figured it was time to call it a day. The thinking was internal; they didn't release Riddick from his contract or make any concrete moves.

**Lou Dibella:** We could clearly see that he was damaged goods after the second Golota fight. I love Riddick Bowe to death but it was obvious that something was wrong. I remember his lawyers using brain injury as an excuse for his change in behavior. Contrary to some opinions, we did not force Bowe to retire. We did not force him to do anything.

Before anything could happen, however, Riddick Bowe made the strangest decision of his career. Riddick Bowe decided he wanted to be in the marines.

With the world awaiting Riddick Bowe's decision, Riddick pulled a rabbit out of his hat. He called a press conference and announced that he was going into the marine corps. The marine corps declaration was every bit as strange as Fan Man. The marines are legendary for their discipline. They wake up early and work all day. The drill sergeants at basic are in your face and relentless. On the surface, it seemed like the last place on earth for Riddick Bowe. The uncanny behavior seemed to represent a change in Riddick Bowe's personality. At the time, no one knew what to make of such a decision.

Ross Greenburg: I remember HBO wanting to resume our relationship with Riddick. Then he came out with that strange marine announcement. We actually did the press conference at HBO because he was one of our guys. He clearly was not the same fighter, but we figured he would come back for another fight. When he left the marines like a week later, the sweat started to mount on our collective brows. We didn't know what we were going to do if he came back and asked us for another fight. The whole marine thing was a blessing in disguise for HBO. It gave us an out. It was a relief to be honest. This had nothing to do with Riddick Bowe personally. He was a sweet wonderful man. He would always give me a big hug every time I saw him. I liked being around him. He just let his life get away from him, it's tragic. In my line of work, I have seen this story replicated plenty of times, and it is sad to see.

Riddick's tour of duty at Parris Island lasted for exactly eleven days. The vigorous nature of the marine regimen was too much for the former champ to handle. A Marine Spokesman told the Chicago Tribune that Riddick Bowe " had been having difficulty adjusting to the regimented lifestyle". Riddick Bowe left Parris Island. He came home to see himself being mocked in the media. It was a tough time. His fight career was in tatters. His wife was leaving him. The year 1996 would mark the end of Riddick Bowe's tenure as a top-flight prizefighter. It was shocking end to a career that just four years earlier looked limitless. There were many factors that contributed to Riddick Bowe's rapid rise and fall.

Larry Merchant: Riddick Bowe is a tragic figure in boxing history. In those first three fights with Holyfield, and then the two fights with Golota, Bowe took more punishment than a heavyweight champion would take in a career. Riddick Bowe took a tremendous number of hard clean shots on his head. He was only twenty-eight and took more accumulated punishment than most fighters take in a career. It was a swift and unfortunate end. Riddick Bowe was one of the great short-term heavyweight champions of all time. If he is not the greatest, he is right there at the top. All the skills and the personality you could ask for. I don't know anyone who was as good as Riddick Bowe that held the title for short amount of time. I am not sure if that is a category in the boxing lexicon. If it is, Bowe belongs at or near the top. When ring historians put together the list of the best heavyweights, Bowe is never on it, I get that, if there is a next category, however, he belongs.

Riddick's life took a nosedive once he left the ring. Riddick's Bowe's marital problems morphed into something much worse. In 1998, Riddick Bowe was arrested and charged with kidnapping his wife and five children with the threat of force. Court documents stated that Riddick also stabbed Judy Bowe in the breast. He allegedly told her he would kill her if he caught her with another man. Riddick Bowe then allegedly forced his family into his vehicle. They took off for Fort Washington, Maryland. The Virginia State Police intervened in South Hills, Virginia. Upon stopping at a McDonald's, Judy Bowe was able to alert the police by telling restaurant employees she was being kidnapped. Riddick Bowe eventually pled guilty to kidnapping and stabbing Judy Bowe. Riddick was facing state and federal charges since he had crossed into another state (Virginia) while he was committing a crime that started in North Carolina. A federal court in Charlotte initially sentenced Riddick to thirty days in prison. Riddick Bowe also received probation. A condition of his probation was that he would not be allowed to box. This particular detail was a result of the defense that Riddick's lawyers used in court. The defense's theory of the crime had psychological implications. Citing brain injuries suffered during his long boxing career, his lawyers contended that brain damage changed Riddick's personality and led him to commit criminal acts.

**Dr. Margaret Goodman:** I have met Riddick a few times the last three times he fought in Las Vegas in 1995 and 1995. I believe that Riddick was an amazingly talented fighter. His boxing career was complicated by issues with weight which affect any fighter's training regimen. Fluctuations in weight and added weight slow a boxer, and I believe this slowed Riddick as time went on and made it more difficult for him to avoid punishment. Increased punishment and blows to the head contribute to chronic brain injury. I believe that towards the end of his career, after the Golata fights, it was clear that Riddick showed evidence of post-concussive symptoms. All one had to do was listen to his interviews right after those bouts. Yes, slurred speech (from head trauma) can improve, to some degree, the longer someone stays away from further head shots. But, allowing Riddick to continue fighting after that time placed him at considerable increased risk of dementia pugilistica.

Yes, Riddick was young to show signs and symptoms, but this is certainly not unheard of. Chronic brain injury that can happen from boxing can cause personality changes in addition to typical symptoms like trouble with memory, concentration, balance, coordination, headaches, confusion... Violent behavior, personality changes, agitation, depression can each be seen with chronic trauma.

If I am not mistaken, Riddick's attorneys used boxing as the reason for his personality changes and aggressive behavior. I believe they even said that he had brain damage as a result of boxing. Following that time, Riddick wished to resume his career and stated these were only methods used by his legal counsel and that he had no brain damage. However, his slurred speech, balance issues and personality changes could have all been from chronic brain injury

The verdict was seen by some as a soft resolution for such a dangerous crime. The backlash prompted prosecutors to appeal the ruling.

Their appeals would bear fruit. Riddick's sentence was overturned and he was sent to federal lockup for eighteen months. The kidnapping charge was the true end of Riddick's boxing career as a top flight heavyweight.. His life would never fully recover. It also took a considerable amount of his money.

Riddick Bowe and Rock Newman had also split ties shortly after his career ended.

**Riddick Bowe:** As soon as I was not worth money to Rock Newman, he was done with me. Suing him may have not been the best idea, but he could have been there for me when I needed him. I was going through a lot when my career ended, and he was not there for me. All he cares about is himself. He did a lot for my career and me, but at the end of the day, where was he when times were difficult? He was nowhere, gone.

The split was ugly and drawn out. Riddick contended that Rock Newman and Spencer Promotions jerked him out of millions. He took his dispute to a higher court. He sued Rock Newman and Spencer Promotions for thirty million dollars only to go back on his filing and actually wrote Rock Newman a letter of apology. The apology letter seemed to make peace between both men. Riddick absolved Rock of any misgivings. He thanked Rock Newman for everything he had done for his boxing career. That peace was about as solid as the Korean Peninsula; the two men broke ties and never mended them. A certain writer spoke with both men, and the acrimony lives large to this day. It's tragic because they both did so much for each other professionally. Pride, ego, and frankly the expiration of financial opportunity decimated their relationship. Among the tragedies of Riddick Bowe, Rock Newman is very high on the list. Riddick Bowe's dire financial situation was not of Rock's making. Rock Newman had made Riddick Bowe a millionaire many times over.

**Richard Steele:** It is unfair to blame Rock Newman for Riddick's financial troubles. I think it's important to point out that Rock did everything he could to give Riddick every advantage. I can remember a conversation that Rock and Riddick had that I was present at. I think they were discussing the details of the third Holyfield fight. Rock asked Riddick how much money he wanted for the fight. Riddick told him six million. Rock got him eight million. Rock was always willing to go the extra mile for Riddick Bowe financially. Rock Newman is a smart guy. He didn't live all lavish with his money, he saved it, invested it. He was a businessman. He invested in baseball teams and did things to ensure his future. It's no surprise that at the end of the day, he was well off and the Riddick was hurting. A fighter spending their entire fortune is a common thing in boxing. It's easy to blame the manager, but it's not always the right thing to do. Rock Newman took care of his money and Riddick Bowe didn't.

Ross Greenburg: Rock Newman deserves a lot of credit for the chances that Riddick Bowe had. He did a masterful job of guiding his career from the Olympics to the fight with Holyfield. He could negotiate his ass off, and he worked hard for Riddick Bowe. He took us for a ride with some of the fights we agreed too. That speaks to his good relationship with Seth Abraham. We were paying a gargantuan amount of money for Riddick Bowe's fights. Way more than we pay for fights today. It's all a testament to Rock Newman. Riddick Bowe was an amazing commodity: personable, warm, gifted American athlete. Do you know what I would give to have that today?

Thell Torrence: It's a lot like Mayweather now; you're so young that you think you are set. When boxing is over, you have to take care of your money. If you don't change your lifestyle, you are going to have trouble. The thing about Bowe was the amount of people that were around him. You try

> to talk to him, and these people push you away. His whole life took a turn for the worst. Everyone in his life was after his money. Riddick was a smart guy; he laid out a plan to prosper, but he made some bad decisions financially. He trusted some bad people; when it was over had had no one to go to. When Rock left, it killed him. He depended on Rock for everything. Now this kid, fresh out of the ghetto, has to do everything by himself.

Riddick Bowe saw the fortune he made in the ring dwindle down to nothing. Between his wife Judy, his family, and legal troubles, the money was not enough to last everyone. Riddick's short and steep fall from grace is about as sad as it gets in the sport. He was a tremendous talent, but he was only champion for a year and left a lot on the table according to most critics. Riddick Bowe's undoing was his personal habits and career decisions. The people around him, the vultures, contributed to his fall, but they do not bear total responsibility. Riddick Bowe would come out of retirement in 2005 to outpoint Billy Zumbrun and told the world that he was back to win the heavyweight title. The fight was fought on the undercard of a card featuring modern-day heavyweight kingpin Vitali Klitschcko. Riddick would only fight two more times, most recently in 2008. Riddick Bowe now lives with his second wife Teri in Fort Washington, Maryland. He works with handicap children and teaches his former craft at LA boxing in Fairfax, Virginia. Riddick's life has been marred by financial problems and personal turmoil. His home, built after he defeated Evander the first time, is in foreclosure. He personally filed for Chapter 7 in 2010. As broke as Riddick Bowe was when he first turned pro, that is about where he stands today while you are reading this. Once upon time, however, he was Big Daddy, the champ. To many, Riddick Bowe's triumphs not his tragedy is what will endure.

**Richard Steele:** Riddick Bowe is the type of person you have to love. Always had a smile on his face and always trying to make people laugh. Kind of a huckster. He was always playing around and prankin' on people. I enjoyed being around him, and I consider him a friend to this day.

Joe Cortez: When Bowe was in his prime, he was an outstanding heavyweight. He was one of if not the best heavyweight that was out there. He could box, he could punch, he had it all. He was great for boxing and was easily one of the best fighters to come out of the heavyweight division in recent times.

# Epilogue

When I first started out, I was not sure how difficult it would be to produce a work worthy of Riddick's boxing career. Time will tell if I hit the mark. No matter what the fallout is, I remain forever grateful to all of the wonderful people that supported my project. I was a boxing fan that became a blogger; I was a blogger that became independent journalist. I have now become an author. I could not have done it without Riddick Bowe. Not just the man but also his story. Sometimes when I was conducting interviews, or reading material, I would realize that Riddick Bowe's boxing career is one of the most interesting stories in all of sports. I feel blessed that he gave me the opportunity to communicate his journey to you, the fans. I am duly aware that there is some things in my book that will cause a stir. To those that will inquire, I simply researched a story and reported upon it without bias. If I turned up some information that bothers you, I am sorry, I had a responsibility to the inquiring public. This is my first book. That unto itself is a miracle. When I was younger, and even into college, I had documented learning disabilities. Specifically, I had a lot of trouble with grammar and punctuation. Still do, he-he. To think that I would go on to write book proves that anything is possible. The best thing to come out of all of writing this book is my friendship with Riddick Bowe. He is a kind, caring man. Everywhere we go, he is mobbed. Being a boxing writer, I talk to boxing fans on a daily basis; and from what I can tell, Riddick Bowe is a highly celebrated fighter. He was not a long-term heavyweight champion, but he did touch the fans. I was among them. I am his fan, his biographer, and his friend. It is my hope that he will find his way and live a long happy life, along with his wonderful wife Teri and their daughter. This book is my thank you to Riddick Bowe. I also want to send some love out to the families of Thell Torrence, Eddie Futch, and Rock Newman. Rock Newman declined to be interviewed for this work; despite that, Rock was very kind and polite when we did speak. I would imagine that when Rock is ready, his version would make one heck of a book as well. I will mention them in the credits, but I am going to give them love anyway.

HBO, by far, was the biggest contributor to my book. Larry Merchant, Jim Lampley, Emanuel Steward, Lou Dibella, and Ross Greenburg, thank you. I also want to thank the people in the HBO archives. Thank you for everything. I have a vision of this book becoming a movie, God willing, that will be the next dream that I realize. I hope you enjoyed the story of Riddick Bowe. As I see it anyway

# Work Cited

I would like to thank the following people for supporting my project. Through email and phone interviews, the following people gave my work credibility, and insight.

Larry Merchant - HBO boxing analyst since 1972

Jim Lampley - HBO boxing blow-by-blow commentator since 1986

Harold Lederman - HBO's unofficial judge

Kathy Duva - CEO of Main Events Promotion

Lou Dibella - Former matchmaker at HBO, now CEO of Dibella Entertainment (want to give a shoutout to my man Alex Dombroff)

Joe Cortez - Hall of Fame referee

Wayne Kelly - Referee for Riddick Bowe-Andrew Golota 1

Angelou Dundee - Hall of Famer trainer, trained Ali

Steve Farhood - Showtime boxing analyst, 2010 winner of the Nat Fleisher award (excellence in boxing journalism)

Thell Torrence - Riddick Bowe's trainer

Freddie Roach - Riddick Bowe's trainer, currently trains Manny Pacquaio and Amir Khan; 2009 trainer of the year

George Ward - Inspector for the New York State Athletic Commission

Lem Satterfield - Boxing scene senior writer, a dear friend

Derek Ginota - Staff writer SecondsOut.com, Like me, he has big plans in this game of boxing

Kieran Mulvaney - ESPN, coolest man ever

Emanuel Steward - Evander Holyfield's trainer, current commentator for HBO

Jerry Roth - Nevada State judge

Chuck Giampa - Nevada State judge

Terry Lane - Boxing promoter, son of Mills Lane

Marc Ratner - Head of the Nevada State Athletic commission, currently top level executive for the UFC (Ultimate Fighting Championship)

Ken Sanders - Evander Holyfield's manager

Shelly Finkel - Boxing manager

Mackie Shilstone - Riddick Bowe's nutritionist

Riddick Bowe - Former two-time heavyweight champion, our protagonist

Evander Holyfield - Former four-time heavyweight champion

Ross Greenburg - President of HBO Sports, a very good man

Zaira Nazario - Boxing insider

Thom Loverro - *Washington Times*

Jeffery Shultz - *Atlanta Journal Constitution*

Richard Steele - Famed boxing referee

Drug Enforcement Administration (DEA)


I would like to also thank the following publications for contributing to my research (indirectly):

*New York Daily News*

*Los Angeles Times*

*Las Vegas Review Journal*

Boxingscene.com

*'ing magazine*

*'o Tribune*

*', Times*

*Washington Times*

*Baltimore Sun*

*Boston Globe*

*Wikipedia*

*Washington Post*

I want to thank the following people. In some way, you inspired me to reach great heights:

James Vick, Beverly Vick, Zach Vick, Crystal Vick, Wendy Vick, Linda Lindroth, Mark Levinstein, Jack McDonald, Eminem, David Haney, Josh Ryeczek, Brian Bishop, David and Amy Burns, Jon Ness, Snakes, Isabel Mulet Romero, Andrew Delory, Jeff Mclean, William Dawson, Kathy Cooke, the crew up at Sunoco esp Corey, the staff at JCCNV, Mike Logan, Tom Simpson, Nicole "Lizzle" Daddario Ryan Blevins, Jimmy Lange, Holly Trexler, Lynnette Lowrimore, Mrs. Greco, my debate club, The Fairfax Celtics, the children and teachers of the Saint Agnes School in Arlington, Virginia, the faculty of Quinnipiac University, for putting up with me and giving me the tools to create this work.